CHRONICLES OF CANADA

Edited by George M. Wrong and H. H. Langton

In thirty-two volumes

32

THE RAILWAY BUILDERS

BY OSCAR D. SKELTON

Part IX

National Highways

'THE SURVEYOR, OFTEN AN EXPLORER AS WELL,
STRIKING OUT INTO THE WILDERNESS IN SEARCH
OF MOUNTAIN PASS OR LOWER GRADE'

From a colour drawing by C. W. Jefferys

THE
RAILWAY BUILDERS

A Chronicle of Overland Highways

BY

OSCAR D. SKELTON

EX UNO
DISCE OMNES

TORONTO

GLASGOW, BROOK & COMPANY

1916

F
1003
C56
vol.32

13939

CONTENTS

		Page
I. THE COMING OF THE RAILWAY	. . .	1
II. EARLY TRAVEL IN CANADA	. . .	13
III. THE CALL FOR THE RAILWAY	. . .	27
IV. THE CANADIAN BEGINNINGS	. . .	36
V. THE GRAND TRUNK ERA	. . .	52
VI. THE INTERCOLONIAL	. . .	93
VII. THE CANADIAN PACIFIC—BEGINNINGS	.	109
VIII. BUILDING THE CANADIAN PACIFIC	.	131
IX. THE ERA OF AMALGAMATION	. .	169
X. THE CANADIAN NORTHERN	. .	181
XI. THE EXPANSION OF THE GRAND TRUNK	.	196
XII. SUNDRY DEVELOPMENTS	. . .	220
XIII. SOME GENERAL QUESTIONS	. .	240
BIBLIOGRAPHICAL NOTE	. . .	248
INDEX	. . . . . .	249

ILLUSTRATIONS

'THE SURVEYOR, OFTEN AN EXPLORER AS WELL, STRIKING OUT INTO THE WILDERNESS IN SEARCH OF MOUNTAIN PASS OR LOWER GRADE'. . *Frontispiece*

From a colour drawing by C. W. Jefferys.

THE FIRST RAILWAY ENGINE IN CANADA, CHAMPLAIN AND ST LAWRENCE RAILROAD, 1837 . . . . *Facing page* 38

From a print in the Château de Ramezay.

RAILROADS AND LOTTERIES . . . . " 48

An Early Canadian Prospectus.

SIR FRANCIS HINCKS . . . . " 66

From a portrait in the Dominion Archives.

RAILWAYS OF BRITISH NORTH AMERICA, 1860 (Map) . . . . " 92

SIR GEORGE SIMPSON . . . . " 110

From a print in the John Ross Robertson Collection, Toronto Public Library.

SIR SANDFORD FLEMING . . . . " 114

From a photograph by Topley.

FLEMING ROUTE AND THE TRANSCONTINENTALS (Map) . . . . " 118

RAILWAYS OF CANADA, 1880 (Map) . *Facing page* 130

LORD STRATHCONA . . . . ,, 134
From a photograph by Lafayette, London.

LORD MOUNT STEPHEN . . . . ,, 140
From a photograph by Wood and Henry, Dufftown. By courtesy of Sir William Van Horne.

SIR WILLIAM CORNELIUS VAN HORNE . ,, 148
From a photograph by Notman.

RAILWAYS OF CANADA, 1896 (Map) . ,, 180

CANADIAN NORTHERN RAILWAY, 1914 (Map) ,, 194

CHARLES MELVILLE HAYS . . ,, 200
From a photograph by Notman.

GRAND TRUNK SYSTEM, 1914 (Map) . . ,, 218

CANADIAN PACIFIC RAILWAY, 1914 (Map) . ,, 224

GREAT NORTHERN RAILWAY, 1914 (Map) . ,, 230

RAILWAYS OF CANADA, 1914 (Map) . . ,, 238

CHAPTER I

THE COMING OF THE RAILWAY

On the morning of October 6, 1829, there began at Rainhill, in England, a contest without parallel in either sport or industry. There were four entries:

Braithwaite and Ericsson's *Novelty*.
Timothy Hackworth's *Sans-pareil*.
Stephenson and Booth's *Rocket*.
Burstall's *Perseverance*.

These were neither race-horses nor stage-coaches, but rival types of the newly invented steam locomotive. To win the £500 prize offered, the successful engine, if weighing six tons, must be able to draw a load of twenty tons at ten miles an hour, and to cover at least seventy miles a day. Little wonder that an eminent Liverpool merchant declared that only a parcel of charlatans could have devised such a test, and wagered that if a locomotive ever went ten miles an hour. he

would eat a stewed engine-wheel for break-
fast !

The contest had come about as the only
solution of a deadlock between the stubborn
directors of the Liverpool and Manchester
Railway, or tramway, then under construction, and their still more stubborn engineer,
one George Stephenson.   The railway was
nearly completed, and the essential question
of the motive power to be used had not yet
been decided.   The most conservative authorities thought it best to stick to the horse ;
others favoured the use of stationary steam-
engines, placed every mile or two along the
route, and hauling the cars from one station
to the next by long ropes ; Stephenson, with
a few backers, urged a trial of the locomotive.
True, on the Stockton and Darlington Railway, the first successful public line ever built,
opened four years before, a Travelling Engine,
built by the same dogged engineer, had hauled
a train of some forty light carriages nearly
nine miles in sixty-five minutes, and had even
beaten a stage-coach, running on the highway
alongside, by a hundred yards in the twelve
miles from Darlington to Stockton.   But even
here the locomotive was only used to haul
freight ; passengers were still carried in old

stage-coaches, which were mounted on special wheels to fit the rails, and were drawn by horses. The best practical engineers in England, when called into consultation, inspected the Stockton road, and then advised the perplexed directors to instal twenty-one stationary engines along the thirty-one miles of track, rather than to experiment with the new Travelling Engine.

'What can be more palpably absurd and ridiculous,' the *Quarterly Review* had declared in 1825, 'than the prospect held out of locomotives travelling twice as fast as stage-coaches! We should as soon expect the people of Woolwich to suffer themselves to be fired off upon one of Congreve's ricochet rockets as trust themselves to the mercy of such a machine, going at such a rate.' And the *Quarterly* was not alone in its scepticism. The directors of the new railway had found great difficulty in obtaining a charter from parliament—a difficulty registered in a bill for parliamentary costs reaching £27,000, or over $4000 a mile. Canal proprietors and toll-road companies had declaimed against the attack on vested rights. Country squires had spluttered over the damage to fox covers. Horses could not plough in neighbouring fields.

Widows' strawberry-beds would be ruined. What would become of coachmen and coach-builders and horse-dealers? 'Or suppose a cow were to stray upon the line; would not that be a very awkward circumstance?' queried a committee member, only to give Stephenson an opening for the classic reply in his slow Northumbrian speech: 'Ay, verra awkward for the coo.' And not only would the locomotive as it shot along do such varied damage; in truth, it would not go at all; the wheels, declared eminent experts, would not grip on the smooth rails, or else the engines would prove top-heavy.

To decide the matter, the directors had offered the prize which brought together the *Novelty*, the *Sans-pareil*, the *Rocket*, and the *Perseverance*, engines which would look almost as strange to a modern crowd as they did to the thousands of spectators drawn up along the track on that momentous morning. The contest was soon decided. The *Novelty*, an ingenious engine but not substantially built, broke down twice. The *Sans-pareil* proved wasteful of coal and also met with an accident. The *Perseverance*, for all its efforts, could do no better than five or six miles an hour. The *Rocket* alone met all requirements. In a seventy-mile run it averaged fifteen miles an hour and reached a maximum of twenty-nine. Years afterwards, when scrapped to a colliery, the veteran engine was still able, in an emergency, to make four miles in four and a half minutes. ' Truly,' declared Cropper, one of the directors who had stood out for the stationary engine and the miles of rope, ' now has George Stephenson at last delivered himself.'

Stephenson had the good fortune, he had earned it indeed, to put the top brick on the wall, and he alone lives in popular memory. But the railway, like most other great inventions, came about by the toil of hundreds of known and unknown workers, each adding his little or great advance, until at last some genius or some plodder, standing on their failures, could reach success. Both the characteristic features of the modern railway, the iron road and the steam motive power, developed gradually as necessity urged and groping experiment permitted.

The iron road came first. When men began to mine coal in the north of England, the need grew clear of better highways to bear the heavy cart-loads to market or riverside. About 1630 one Master Beaumont laid down broad wooden rails near Newcastle, on which a single horse could haul fifty or sixty bushels of coal. The new device spread rapidly through the whole Tyneside coal-field. A century later it became the custom to nail thin strips of wrought iron to the wooden rails, and about 1767 cast-iron rails were first used. Carr, a Sheffield colliery manager, invented a flanged rail, while Jessop, another colliery engineer, took the other line by using flat rails but flanged cart-wheels. The outburst of canal building in the last quarter of the eighteenth century overshadowed for a time the growth of the iron road, but it soon became clear that the 'tramway' was necessary to supplement, if not to complete, the canal. In 1801 the first public line, the Surrey Iron Railway, was chartered, but it was not until 1825 that the success of the Stockton and Darlington Railway proved that the iron way could be made as useful to the general shipping public as to the colliery owner. At the outset this road was regarded as only a special sort of toll-road upon which any carrier might transport goods or passengers in his own vehicles, but experience speedily made it necessary for the company to undertake the complete service.

It took longer to find the new motive power,

but this, too, first came into practical use in the land where peace and liberty gave industry the fostering care which the war-rent Continent could never guarantee. Nowadays it seems a simple thing to turn heat energy into mechanical energy, to utilize the familiar expansive power of water heated to vapour. Yet centuries of experiment, slowly acquired mechanical dexterity, and an industrial atmosphere were needed for the development of the steam-engine, and later of the locomotive. Inventiveness was not lacking in the earlier days. In the second century before Christ, Hero of Alexandria had devised steam fountains and steam turbines, but they remained scientific toys, unless for the miracle-working purposes to which legend says that eastern priests adapted them. So in the seventeenth century, when the Norman, Solomon de Caus, claimed that with the vapour of boiling water he could move carriages and navigate ships, Cardinal Richelieu had him put in prison as a madman. About 1628 an Italian, Giovanni Branca, invented an engine which had the essential features of the modern turbine, but his crude apparatus lacked efficiency.

Once more the coal-mines of England set invention working on a definite, continuous object. As the shafts were sunk to lower and lower levels, it became impossible to pump the water out of the mines by horse power, and the aid of steam was sought. Just at the close of the seventeenth century Savery devised the first commercial steam-engine, or rather steam fountain, which applied cold water to the outside of the cylinder to condense the steam inside and produce a vacuum; while Papin, one of the Huguenot refugees to whom industrial England owed so much, planned the first cylinder and piston engine. Then in 1705 Newcomen and Cawley, working with Savery, took up Papin's idea, separated boiler from cylinder, and thus produced a vacuum into which atmospheric pressure forced the piston and worked the pump. Next Humphrey Potter, a youngster hired to open and shut the valves of a New-comen engine, made it self-acting by tying cords to the engine-beam, had his hour for play or idling, and proved that if necessity is the mother of invention, laziness is sometimes its father. Half a century passed without material advance; even as perfected in detail by Smeaton, the Newcomen engine required thirty-five pounds of coal to produce one horse-power per hour, as against one pound to-day. Then James Watt, instrument-maker in Glasgow, seeing that much of the waste of steam was due to the alternate chilling and heating of the cylinder, added a separate condenser in which to do the chilling, and kept the temperature of the cylinder uniform by applying a steam-jacket. Later, by applying steam and a vacuum to each side of the piston alternately, and by other improvements, Watt, with his partner Boulton, brought the reciprocating steam-engine to a high stage of efficiency.

It took fifty years longer to combine the steam - engine and the rail. French and American inventors devised steam carriages, which came to nothing. England again led the way. At Redruth in Cornwall Boulton and Watt had a branch for the erection of stationary engines in Cornish tin-mines, in charge of William Murdock, later known as inventor of the system of lighting by gas. Murdock devised a steam carriage to run upon the ordinary highway, but was discouraged by his employers from perfecting the machine. Another mechanic at Redruth, Richard Trevithick, captain in a tin-mine, took up the torch, built a ' Dragon ' for use on the common highway, but was baffled by the hopeless badness of the roads, and turned to making a locomotive for use on the iron ways of the Welsh collieries. Two years later, in 1803, he had constructed an ingenious engine, which could haul a ten-ton load five miles an hour, but the engine jolted the road to pieces, and the versatile inventor was diverted to other schemes. Blenkinsop of Leeds in 1812 had an engine built with a toothed wheel working in a racked rail, which did years of good service; and next year at Wylam on the Tyne a colliery owner, Blackett, had the *Puffing Billy* built, and proved that smooth wheels would grip smooth rails. Still another year, and an engine-wright in a Tyneside colliery, George Stephenson, himself born at Wylam, devised the *Blücher*, doubling effectiveness by turning the exhaust steam into the chimney to create a strong draught. Using this steam blast, and adopting the multitubular boiler from a French inventor, Seguin, Stephenson finally scored a triumph, due not so much to unparalleled genius as to dogged perseverance in working out his own ideas and in adapting the ideas of other men.

Thus by slow steps the steam railway had come. It was a necessity of the age. Crude means of transport might serve the need of

earlier days when each district was self-con-
tained and self-sufficing. But now the small
workshop and the craftsman's tool were giving way to the huge factory and the power-
driven machine. The division of labour was
growing more complex. Each district was
becoming more dependent on others for
markets in which to buy and to sell. Traffic
was multiplying. The industrial revolution
brought the railway, and the railway quickened the pace of the industrial revolution.

To some critics, as to Ruskin, railways have
appeared ' the loathesomest form of deviltry
now extant, animated and deliberate earthquakes, destructive of all nice social habits
or possible natural beauty.' Animated and
deliberate earthquakes they were indeed to
prove, transforming social and industrial and
political structures the world over. With the
telegraph and the telephone, they greatly
widened the scope and quickened the pace of
business operations, making it possible, and
therefore necessary, for the captain of industry or finance of the twentieth century to
have under control ten times the press of
affairs which occupied his eighteenth-century
forerunner. The railway levelled prices and
levelled manners. It enabled floods of settlers

to sweep into all the waste places of the earth, clamped far-flung nations into unity, and bound country to country.

Nowhere was the part played so momentous as in the vast spaces of the North American continent, and not least in the northern half. The railway found Canada scarcely a geographical expression, and made it a nation.

CHAPTER II

EARLY TRAVEL IN CANADA

BRITISH NORTH AMERICA before the railway came was a string of scattered provinces. Lake Huron was the western boundary of effective settlement: beyond lay the fur trader's preserve. Between Upper and Lower Canada and the provinces by the Atlantic a wilderness intervened. With the peninsula of Ontario jutting southwest between Michigan and New York, and the northeastern states of the Union thrusting their borders nearly to the St Lawrence, the inland and the maritime provinces knew less of each other than of the neighbouring states.

Settlement clung close to river, lake, and sea. Till the Eastern Townships were settled, Lower Canada had been one long-drawn-out village with houses close set on each side of the river streets. Deep forest covered all the land save where the lumberman or settler had cut a narrow clearing or fire had left a black-ened waste. To cut roads through swamp and forest and over river and ravine demanded capital, surplus time, and strong and efficient governments, all beyond the possibilities of early days. On the other hand, the waterways offered easy paths. The St Lawrence and the St John and all their tributaries and lesser rivals provided inevitably the points of settlement and the lines of travel.

The development of water transport in Canada furnishes a record of the interaction of route and cargo, of need and invention, of enterprise and capital. First came the bark canoe, quick to build, light to carry round the frequent gaps in navigation, and large enough to hold the few voyageurs or the rich-in-little peltry that were chief cargo in early days. It was the bark canoe that carried explorer, trader, soldier, missionary, and settler to the uttermost north and south and west. For the far journeys it long held its place. Well on into the nineteenth century fur traders were still sending in supplies from Montreal and bringing back peltry from Fort William in flotillas of great bark canoes. For shorter voyages the canoe gave place to the larger and clumsier bateau, the characteristic eighteenth-century conveyance. After the War of 1812 the increasingly heavy downward freight of grain and potash led to the introduction from the United States of the still larger Durham boats. Along the coast and on the Great Lakes the sailing schooner long filled a notable place. Finally the steamboat came. In 1809, only one year after the *Clermont* had begun its regular trips on the Hudson, and before any steamboat plied in British home waters, John Molson of Montreal with John Bruce and John Jackson—luckily for Canada not all three baptized ' Algernon '—built at Montreal the 40-ton steamer *Accommodation*. Seven years later Upper Canada's first steamboat was launched, the 740-ton *Frontenac*, built at the then thriving village of Ernestown. The fleet of river and lake steamers multiplied rapidly. The speed and certainty and comfort—relative, at least—of the steamboat at once gave a forceful impetus to settlement and to travel, and for some sections ended the pioneer period.

Meanwhile, the waterways were being improved. Little was needed or done in the great network of New Brunswick's rivers or in Nova Scotia's shorter streams, but on the St Lawrence system, with a fall of nearly six hundred feet from Lake Erie to tide-water at

Three Rivers, canal construction was imperative. As early as 1779 canals were built round the rapids between Lake St Louis and Lake St Francis, on the St Lawrence, with a depth of only a foot and a half of water on the sills. Far westward, at Sault Ste Marie, the energetic North-West Company built, about 1800, a canal half a mile long. In the early twenties, after the failure of a private company, the province of Lower Canada constructed a boat canal between Montreal and Lachine, and a less successful beginning was made on a canal round the Chambly rapids on the Richelieu. In Upper Canada the British government built the Rideau Canal, chiefly for military purposes. The Welland Canal was begun by a private company in 1824, opened for small boats five years later, and taken over by the province in 1840, after a record notable alike for energy and perseverance and for jobbery and inefficiency. After the Union of 1841, when population, revenue, and credit were all growing, energetic digging was begun on the St Lawrence system of canals, and by 1848 vessels of twenty-six foot beam and drawing nine feet of water could sail from the ocean to Chicago.

Land transport came later than water transport, and developed by slower stages. Road-making was an art which the settler learned slowly. The blazed trail through the woods sufficed for the visit to the neighbour or the church, or for the tramp to the nearest grist-mill with a sack of wheat on one's back. ' He who has been once to church and twice to mill is a traveller,' the common saying ran. The trail broadened to a bridle-road for pack-horse or saddle-horse. The winter, that maligned stepmother of Canada, gave the settler an excellent though fleeting road on the surface of the frozen river or across the hard-packed snow. Through the endless swamps jolting ' corduroy ' roads were built of logs laid crosswise on little or no foundation. With more hands and more money there came the graded road, fenced and bridged, but more rarely gravelled. Finally, little earlier than the railway, came the macadamized road, and that peculiar invention of Upper Canada, the plank road, built of planks laid crosswise on a level way, and covered with earth to lessen the wear and noise. Upon these roads carriole or calèche, ' cutter ' or ' lumber-wagon,' carried the settler or his goods to meeting-place and market. By 1816 a stage route was estab-lished from Montreal to Kingston, a year later from Kingston to York (Toronto), and in 1826 from Toronto to Niagara and from Ancaster to Detroit.

Road-making policy fluctuated between the Scylla of local neglect and the Charybdis of centralized jobbery. At first the settler was burdened with the task of clearing roughly the road in front of his own land, but the existence of vast tracts of Clergy Reserves, or other grants exempt from clearing duties, made this an ineffective system. Labour on roads required by statute, whether shared equally by all settlers or allotted according to assessed property, proved little more successful. On the other hand, the system of provincial grants for road-building too often meant log-rolling and corruption, and in the Canadas it was discontinued after the establishment of municipal institutions in 1841. The reaction to local control was perhaps too extreme, and we are to-day recognizing the need of more aid and control by the central provincial authorities. In the Maritime Provinces the system worked better, and when the railway came these provinces possessed a good network of great roads and by-roads, without a single toll-gate. With the passing of the Joint Stock Act by the Canadian legislature in 1849, toll-road companies were freely organized, and many of the leading roads were sold by the government to these private corporations, and without question their operations brought marked improvement for a time.

To realize more concretely the mode of travelling before the railway came, let us make the journey, say, from Quebec to Toronto, at three different periods, in 1800, in 1830, and in 1850.

'In no part of North America,' wrote an experienced traveller just at the close of the eighteenth century, 'can a traveller proceed so commodiously as along the road from Quebec to Montreal.'[1] A posting service had been established which could fairly be compared with European standards. At regular intervals along the road the traveller found post-houses, where the post-master kept four vehicles in readiness : in summer the calèche, a one-horse chaise built for two passengers, with a footboard seat for the driver and with the body hung by broad leather straps or thongs of bull's hide ; in winter the carriole, or sledge, with or without

[1] Isaac Weld, *Travels through the States of North America and the Provinces of Upper and Lower Canada* (Fourth Edition), p. 300.

covered top, also holding two passengers and a driver. The drivers were bound to make two leagues an hour over the indifferent roads, and in midwinter and midsummer the dexterous, talkative, good-humoured driver, or *marche-donc*, usually exceeded this rate for most of the journey of three days. From Montreal onward no one travelled in winter except an occasional Indian messenger. Even in summer few thought of going by land, though some half-broken trails stretched westward. The river was the king's highway. The summer traveller at once purchased the equipment needed for a week's river journey —tent, buffalo-skins, cooking utensils, meat and drink—and secured passage on board one of the bateaux which went up the river at irregular intervals in brigades of half a dozen. The bateau was a large flat-bottomed boat, built sharp both at bow and stern, with movable mast, square sail, and cross benches for the crew of five or six. Sometimes an awning or small cabin provided shelter. In still water or light current the French-Canadian crew—always merry, sometimes sober, singing their voyageur songs, halting regularly for the inevitable ' pipe '—rowed or sailed ; where the current was strong they

kept inshore and pushed slowly along by
'setting' poles, eight or ten feet long and
iron shod ; and where the rapids grew too
swift for poling, the crews joined forces on
the shore to haul each bateau in turn by long
ropes, while the passengers lent a hand or shot
wild pigeons in the neighbouring woods. At
night the whole party encamped on shore,
erecting tents or hanging skins and boughs
from branches of friendly trees. With average
weather Kingston could be reached in seven
or eight days ; the return journey down-stream
was made in two or three. From Kingston
westward the journey was continued in a sailing schooner, either one of the government
gunboats or a private venture, as far as York,
or even to the greater western metropolis,
Queenston on the Niagara river. In good
weather thirty or forty hours sufficed for the
lake voyage, but with adverse winds from
four to six days were frequently required.

Thirty years later those to whom time or
comfort meant more than money could make
the through journey in one-third the time,
though for the leaner-pursed the more primi-
tive facilities still lingered. For the summer
trip from Quebec to Montreal the steamer
had outstripped the stage-coach. Even with

frequent stops to load the fifty or sixty cords of pine burned on each trip—how many Canadian business men secured their start in prosperity by supplying wood to steamers on lake or river !—the steamer commonly made the hundred and eighty miles in twenty-eight hours. The fares were usually twenty shillings cabin and five shillings steerage, though the intense rivalry of opposing companies sometimes brought reckless rate-cutting. In 1829, for instance, each of the two companies had one boat which carried and boarded cabin passengers for seven and six-pence, while deck passengers who found themselves in food were crowded in for a shilling.

From Montreal to Lachine the well-to-do traveller took a stage-coach, drawn by four spanking greys, leaving Montreal at five in the morning, for stage-coach hours were early and long. At Lachine he left the stage for the steamer, at the Cascades he took a stage again, and at Côteau transferred once more to a steamer for the run to Cornwall. Shortly after 1830 steamers were put on the river powerful enough to breast the current as far as Dickenson's Landing, leaving only a twelve-mile gap to be filled by stage, but in 1830 it was still necessary, if one scorned the bateau, to make the whole journey from Cornwall to Prescott by land, over one of the worst through roads in the province. The Canadian stage of the day was a wonderful contrivance, a heavy lumbering box, slung on leather straps instead of springs, and often made without doors in order that, when fording bridgeless streams, the water might not flow in. With the window as the only means of exit, heavy-built passengers found it some-what awkward when called upon, as they often were, to clamber out in order to ease the load uphill, or to wait while oxen from a neighbouring farm dragged the stage out of a mud-hole. The traveller who ' knew the ropes ' provided himself with buffalo-skins or cushions ; others went without. Arrived at Prescott, the passengers shifted to a river steamer, fitted more commodiously than the little boats used in the lower stretches, but still providing no sleeping quarters except in open bunks circling round the dining-saloon.

For thousands of the immigrants who were pouring into Upper Canada the fares of the river steamer were still prohibitive. Many came on bateaux, sometimes poled along as of yore, sometimes taken in tow by a steamer. Often more than a hundred immigrants, men, women, and children, would be crowded into a single thirty-foot bateau, ' huddled together,' a traveller notes, ' as close as captives in a slave trader, exposed to the sun's rays by day, and the river damp by night, without protection.' [1] Still more used the Durham boat for the river journey. This famous craft was a large, flat-bottomed barge, with round bow and square stern. With centre-board down and mainsail and topsail set on its fixed mast, it made fair progress in the wider stretches. But on the up trip it was for the most part poled or ' set ' along. Each of the crew took his stand at the bow end of one of the narrow gangways which ran along both sides of the boat, set firmly in the river bottom his long, heavy, iron-shod pole, put his shoulder to it, and, bending almost double, walked along the gangway to the stern and inch by inch forced the boat up-stream. ' The noise made by the clanking of the iron against the stones, as the poles were drawn up again toward the bow, could be heard for a long distance on a calm summer's day.' Finally, at Prescott or Kingston the Durham boat was exchanged for

[1] Shirreff, *A Tour through North America*, p. 143.

the lower decks of the steamer, and the rest of the journey made with somewhat greater speed, if not much greater comfort.

The twenty years which followed 1830 saw the steamboat in its prime. The traveller going westward from Quebec in 1850 had a simple task before him : a change at Montreal was the only necessary break in a relatively comfortable and speedy journey. Two days now sufficed for the trip from Montreal to Toronto. In the United States, river boats had been evolved which far surpassed anything Europe had to offer in luxury and speed. Canadian business men were not far behind, and the St Lawrence lake and river route was well supplied with crack steamers, of the Royal Mail and rival lines, or with independent boats. The competition was at times intense, both in fares and in speed. Many Canadians of the day, absorbed in the local or personal rivalries of these boats, and impressed by their magnificence and reliability, were convinced that the last word in transportation had been said. Yet, on the lake and river, winter barred all through traffic. The main turnpike roads of the interior were greatly improved, but even on these long-distance traffic was expensive, and the by-roads, especially in the spring and autumn, were impassable except at a snail's pace. For traffic of town with town and province with province some means of transport less dependent on time and tide was urgently needed.

CHAPTER III

THE CALL FOR THE RAILWAY

WE have seen how in England a succession of workers almost apostolic in continuity had brought the steam railway to practical success, and how in Canada, before the railway came, men were making shift with bateau and steamer, with stage-coach and cart and calèche, to carry themselves and their wares to meeting-place and market. Now we may glance for a moment at the chief hope and motive of those who brought the locomotive across the seas.

In all but the very earliest years of railway planning and building in Canada, two aims have been dominant. One has been political, the desire to clamp together the settlements scattered across the continent, to fill the waste spaces and thus secure the physical basis for national unity and strength. The other has been commercial, the desire to capture the trade and traffic of an ever-expanding and ever-receding west. Local convenience and local interests have played their part, but in the larger strategy of railway building the dominant motives have been political and commercial. They have been blended in varying proportions ; each has acted against the other as well as with it, but at all times they give the key to facts which otherwise remain a meaningless jumble of dates and figures.

The political motive is familiar and needs only brief reference. That the present Canada is not a natural geographical unit is an undeniable fact. Each of the principal sections has more natural connection with the corresponding section of the United States than with the other parts of Canada. And sixty years ago it was doubtful whether any common sentiment could take the place of the physical unity which was lacking. There was, of course, no national consciousness, based on common history and common aspirations. At best the link of the scattered colonies was that of common loyalty to the British crown, and at worst a common inherited antagonism to the great republic to the south. Yet farseeing and courageous men were not content to accept the decrees of geography or of the diplomats who had been over-generous in conceding territory to American claims. They sought unity and understanding, out of fear of aggression from their overshadowing neighbours and out of faintly shaping hope of what the northern half-continent might become.

For unity, knowledge and daily intercourse were needed ; for knowledge and intercourse, speedy and cheap transportation was essential. Within each province and between the two Canadas much had been done, but neither river, canal, nor turnpike could serve to annihilate the vast distances that separated east from west and west from farthest west. Only the railway could achieve such a task.

But more was needed than patriotic sentiment. All-red speeches might adorn a banquet or win an election, but facts—or fictions —as to freight and dividends were needed to beguile the capital from investors' pockets. The hope of securing for the Canadian provinces the trade and traffic of the golden West was, in early years as in late, much the strongest factor in railway policy.

When the white man came to North America, he found himself hemmed in to the Atlantic coast by the long range of the Appalachians. These mountains, though not lofty, were rugged and covered with dense forests and tangled undergrowth. There were few doorways to the great open spaces beyond. On the far north the southward intrusion of the ocean, known as Hudson Bay, opened a precarious way, important in the early days of the white man's period, possibly to become important again in our own, but negligible during the intervening years. From the south, entrance could be had by the Mississippi and its tributaries, offering for most of the year ten thousand miles of navigable waters. In the east the St Lawrence system, stretching three thousand miles westward from the sea, and the Hudson and Mohawk rivers, passing through a gap in the Alleghanies, offered still more convenient access.

Early and late in the history of the white man's America the land and the trade of the interior have been the prize sought by rival nations and rival cities, and the possession of a speedy and convenient route has been the means of securing the prize. The later warfare was less spectacular than the old, but no less keen. The navvy took the place of the Indian, pick and shovel and theodolite the place of bow and musket, and a lower freight

by a cent on a bushel of wheat became the
ammunition in place of the former glass beads
or fire - water. But seventeenth- or eighteenth-century Englishmen and Frenchmen on
Hudson Bay, Spaniards and Frenchmen on the
Mississippi, Frenchmen and Englishmen on the
St Lawrence, Dutchmen and Englishmen on
the Hudson, did not strive more eagerly for
control than the Montreal and Halifax, Portland and Boston and New York, Philadelphia
and Baltimore and New Orleans of the nineteenth century. The struggle became especially intense when the advancing flood of
settlers cut their way through the Appalachian
woods and burst into the prairies of the
Mississippi valley. There was no longer a ten-
year struggle to clear a space of forty or fifty
acres ; at once the soil was ready for the
plough. For a few years the grain of the
valley states was needed for their own in-
rushing settlers, but a surplus grew rapidly
and had to find an outlet in the east or in
Europe. The miraculous speed of western
settlement and the magnitude of the prize at
stake soon centred public interest on the
question of the route which was to provide
this outlet.

The Mississippi route was the first to be

developed. In canoe and pirogue, bateau, flatboat, and ark, settlers went up and produce came down. But the winding stream, the shifting channel, the swift current, the frequent snag and sand-bar made navigation down-stream dangerous and navigation upstream incredibly slow : the heavier vessels took three months for the trip from New Orleans to Louisville. With the coming of the steamboat a strong impetus was given alike to settlement and to export trade. By the forties New Orleans ranked the fourth port in the world and the Mississippi valley exceeded the British Isles in the ownership of ships' tonnage. In 1850 the Mississippi still carried to the sea cargoes twice the value of those that sought the Lakes and the Erie Canal, though in the import trade these proportions were reversed. At this time a line drawn east and west through the centre of Ohio marked the commercial watershed. Not until after the Civil War did the glories of the Mississippi pass away.

Next, New York devised its master-stroke, the Erie Canal. Gouverneur Morris and De Witt Clinton saw the opportunity which the Mohawk-Hudson cleft in the Appalachian barrier offered, and the state rose to it.

Digging was begun in 1817, and in 1825 the first barge passed from Lake Erie to the Hudson. At first the canal was only a four-foot ditch, but it proved the greatest single factor in the development of the region south of the Lakes. Prosperous cities—Buffalo, Lockport, Rochester, Syracuse, Utica, Schenectady—sprang up all along the route. Cost of transport from Buffalo to New York was cut in four. The success of New York led Pennsylvania to build canals through the state to Pittsburg, with a portage railroad over the Alleghanies, while in the west canals were dug to connect Lake Erie with the Ohio, and Lake Michigan with the Illinois and the Mississippi.

To the Canadian of that day the West meant Upper Canada or Canada West, and ' the far west' meant Illinois and Indiana. The Saskatchewan was to him little more than the Yang-tse-Kiang. But although the far west was not under his own flag, it dominated his thoughts as greatly as the North-West has dominated our thoughts half a century later. Canada sought its share of the western trade. The Canadian provinces were thinly peopled, their revenues were scanty and their credit low, but the example of New York stirred them to the effort to remove the barriers to

navigation in the St Lawrence, and to offer
their magnificent lake and river ship-route
against the petty barge canal which was cap-
turing the western trade.   The Welland Canal
was built to carry east-bound traffic beyond the
point where Buffalo tapped it, and by 1848,
as we have seen, canals were completed on the
St Lawrence, providing a nine-foot waterway
from Chicago to Montreal.

It was a magnificent effort for a struggling colony.   But it was scarcely finished—
the pæans of self-congratulation on the unexpected discovery of an enterprise quite
Yankee in its daring were still echoing—
when it was found to have been made largely
in vain.   So far from monopolizing the trade
of the western states, the St Lawrence route
was not even keeping the east-bound traffic
of Upper Canada itself.   The reasons were
soon plain.   The repeal in 1846 of the Corn
Laws and in 1848 of the differential duties in
favour of the St Lawrence route were temporary blows.   The granting of bonding privileges by the United States in 1845 drew traffic
from Canada to southern routes.   Ocean rates
were cheaper from New York than from
Montreal; in 1850, for example, the freight
on a barrel of flour from New York to

Liverpool was 1s. 3½d., while from Montreal it was 3s. 0½d. This was because the majority of the vessels arriving at Montreal came in ballast, and also because on the outward voyage the offerings of timber made rates high. Timber enjoyed a preference in the British market, and, as has happened since, this preference was simply absorbed by the vessel owner. But most important of all, in the United States the railway, with its speedy, all-year service, had already taken the place of the canal. The Canadian ports were fighting with weapons obsolete before completed.

CHAPTER IV

THE CANADIAN BEGINNINGS

FROM the beginning in Canada, to a much greater degree than in Great Britain or in the United States, the railway was designed to serve through traffic. But it was regarded at first as only a very minor link in the chain. River and canal were still considered the great highways of through traffic. Only where there were gaps to be bridged between the more important waterways was the railway at first thought profitable. In the phrase of one of the most distinguished of Canadian engineers, Thomas C. Keefer, the early roads were portage roads.

In 1832, two years after the completion of the Liverpool and Manchester Railway, a charter was granted by the legislature of Lower Canada to the Company of the Proprietors of the Champlain and St Lawrence Railroad, for a line from Laprairie on the St Lawrence to St Johns, sixteen miles distant on the Richelieu river, just above the rapids. From St Johns transportation to New York was easily effected, through the Richelieu to Lake Champlain and thence to the Hudson. This portage road promised to shorten materially the journey from Montreal to New York.

Construction was begun in 1835, and the road opened for traffic in July 1836. The rails were of wood, with thin flat bars of iron spiked on. These were apt to curl up on the least provocation, whence came their popular name of ' snake-rails.' At first horse power was used, but in 1837 the proprietors imported an engine and an engineer from England. Some premonition of trouble made the management decide to make the trial run by moonlight. In spite of all the efforts of engineer and officials, the *Kitten* would not budge an inch. Finally an engineer, borrowed from the Baltimore and Ohio Railroad, reported that all that was needed was ' more wood and water,' and given these the *Kitten* gambolled along at twenty miles an hour.

The Champlain and St Lawrence was at first operated only in the summer, when its services as a portage route were most needed. After a decade of moderately successful working, it was decided, significantly, to lengthen the rail and shorten the water section of the route. By 1852 the rails had been extended northward to St Lambert, opposite Montreal, and southward to Rouse's Point, on Lake Champlain. Twenty years later this pioneer road, after a period of leasing, was completely absorbed by the Grand Trunk Railway.

For ten years the sixteen-mile Champlain and St Lawrence was the sole steam railway in British North America, while by 1846 the United Kingdom had built over twenty-eight hundred miles, and the United States nearly five thousand. Political unrest, commercial depression, absorption of public funds in canals, hindered development in Canada. Many projects were formed and charters secured—for roads in the western peninsula of Upper Canada, between Cobourg and Rice Lake, on the Upper Ottawa, in the Eastern Townships, and elsewhere—but they all came to nothing. It was not until the railway mania broke out in England in the middle forties—when ' King ' Hudson, first of the great promoters and speculators, turned all to gold; when ninety schemes were floated in a single week, calling for eighty million pounds; when companies capitalized at over seven hundred millions scrambled for charters

THE FIRST RAILWAY ENGINE IN CANADA

CHAMPLAIN AND ST LAWRENCE RAILROAD, 1837

From a print in the Château de Ramezay

and all England fought for their shares—that Canadian promoters found interest awakened and capitalists keen to listen. At the same time, the active competition of United States roads for the western traffic and the approaching completion of the St Lawrence canal system prompted further steps. A second stage in Canadian railway building had begun.

First may be noted three small lines, which were in their beginnings chiefly portage roads of the most limited type. The Montreal and Lachine, begun in 1846 and completed in 1847, was the second complete road built. Its track of eight miles took the place of the earlier stage route round the Lachine rapids. Five years later an extension, the Lake St Louis and Province Line, was built from Caughnawaga, on the opposite shore of the St Lawrence, to the boundary and beyond to Mooer's Junction, where it made connection with American roads, and thus offered a route from Montreal to New York rivalling the older Champlain and St Lawrence route. A steam ferry, which could carry a locomotive and three loaded cars, was used for crossing from Lachine to Caughnawaga. The enlarged line, known as the Montreal and New York Railroad, did not prosper, and was eventually absorbed by its rival, the Champlain and St Lawrence. The third completed road, the St Lawrence and Industry Village, was also built in Lower Canada, running from Lanoraie on the north bank of the St Lawrence twelve miles to the village of Industry, later Joliette. It was opened for traffic in 1850, and was a road for use in summer only. Meanwhile, the desirability of building a road to circumvent Niagara had not escaped attention. In 1835 the Erie and Ontario Railroad was chartered, and in 1839 the line was opened from Queenston to Chippawa. The grades near Queenston were too steep for the locomotives of the day, and the road was operated by horses; even so, it halted a hundred feet above the level of the river, and failed to make good its promise as an effective portage route. In 1852 the charter was amended, and two years later the road was rebuilt from Chippawa to Niagara-on-the-Lake, and operated by steam. It was later extended to Fort Erie and absorbed by the Canada Southern.

More ambitious schemes were under way —the planning of the St Lawrence and Atlantic in Canada East, and of the Great Western and later the Northern in Canada

West. These roads were all designed to secure for Canadian routes and Canadian ports a share of the through traffic of the West. They were all links in longer chains ; the time of independent through roads had not yet come. The St Lawrence and Atlantic was built to secure the supremacy of the upper St Lawrence route by giving Montreal a winter outlet at Portland. The Northern, running from Lake Ontario at Toronto to Georgian Bay at Collingwood, was a magnified portage road, shortening by hundreds of miles the distance from Chicago and the upper lakes to the St Lawrence ports. The Great Western, connecting Buffalo and Detroit, was the central link in the shortest route between New York and Chicago. Not only were these roads important in themselves, but the experience acquired in the endeavour to finance and construct them largely determined the policy of the great era of railway construction which began with the chartering of the Grand Trunk.

The St Lawrence and Atlantic was the Canadian half of the first international railway ever built. At the outset much more than half of the enterprise and activity was centred in the United States, for the Canadas were still apprentices in railway promotion and construction. The ambition of an American seaport prompted the planning of the line, the untiring energy of an American promoter made it possible, and American contractors built the greater part.

The little city of Portland possessed the most northerly harbour on the Atlantic coast of the United States. Mr John A. Poor, whose lifetime was devoted to the extension of railways in northern New England, dreamed of making it, by a road to Montreal, the outlet of the trade of the West, at least so far as freight traffic went. Passengers and mails, he conceived, could best be carried to Europe from Halifax, nearly six hundred miles nearer than New York to Liverpool, but the railway connecting Halifax with the large American cities should pass through Portland, and thus make it an important divisional point, if not a terminus. His enthusiasm fired his fellow-citizens : the city subscribed for stock in the proposed road to Montreal, and guaranteed bonds, while private subscriptions mounted still higher, at least on paper. More difficulty was experienced in inducing allies in Montreal to undertake the Canadian half of the road. Before 1845, however, Montreal business men were convinced that a railway to Portland or Boston offered them the best means of recovering from the blow inflicted by the repeal of the British preference on Canadian wheat and flour. If Montreal could not be the New York of Canada, it might at least occupy the position which Buffalo was now achieving, gathering all the trade of the interior to forward it in summer and especially in winter over the new road. The advantage of such a line in the development of the Eastern Townships was also evident.

The only question in dispute in Canada was as to the relative merits of the Boston and the Portland route. The superior energy of the Portland promoters weighed down the scale in favour of their city. In February 1845 Poor struggled five days through a north-east blizzard, and reached Montreal just in time to turn the vote of the Board of Trade against Boston. He organized a spectacular race of express sleighs to disprove the claim that, though the British packet called at Portland before going on to Boston, the route by Boston would prove speedier. Relays of teams were provided all along the rival roads from Boston and from Portland, five to fifteen miles apart ; evergreen bushes were set up in the snow to mark the road, part of the Montreal mail was taken off at Portland, and part at Boston, and dispatched by the rival couriers. The Portland relay covered the distance, nearly three hundred miles, in twenty hours, and dashed into Montreal, with all colours flying, twelve hours ahead of the Boston contingent. The cheers that greeted the victors marked the definite turn of popular favour toward the Portland route. Two allied companies were incorporated—the Atlantic and St Lawrence to build the United States section of the railway, and the St Lawrence and Atlantic to build from Montreal to the border.

The St Lawrence and Atlantic was a valuable medium of experience, if not of traffic. In its management were found the leading business men of Montreal, such as Moffat, M'Gill, Molson, Stayner, and Torrance. At first all was fair. Subscriptions came in freely from Montreal and the Eastern Townships. One of the youngest of the directors, Alexander T. Galt, then commissioner of the British-American Land Company, succeeded in floating a large quantity of stock in England—the first of countless railway appeals to the London market—only to have the subscriptions with-

drawn in 1846 when the Hudson bubble burst.
The Canadian stockholders put up what money
they could. The city of Montreal took
£125,000 stock. The British-American Land
Company and the Montreal Seminary each lent
£25,000. Country subscribers were permitted
to make payments in pork or eggs for the
use of the construction gang, though one
director resigned because not allowed to turn
in his farm. The contractors, Black, Wood
and Company, as was customary in the
United States at the time, took a large portion
of their payment in stock. Still, funds were
lacking. Internal difficulties developed; directors did not direct; and in 1849 the finances
were found to be in a hopelessly tangled
state. Galt then took charge as president,
with John Young—forwarder and born promoter, active in all transportation schemes,
whether for canal, railway, or bridge—as
vice-president. Under their skilful financing
the work went on, but scarcely forty miles
could be opened in 1849. To complete the
road to the border, in the depression which
prevailed, seemed utterly beyond the unaided
resources of private capitalists, and the directors turned to the government for aid.

Meanwhile, Upper Canada lagged in action,

although schemes were many. Omitting merely local projects, the roads most in the public eye were those leading west and north from Lake Ontario. The Great Western project had been longest under way, and showed a significant evolution. In 1834 the legislature of Upper Canada had granted a charter to the London and Gore Railroad Company. This road was designed to carry the products of the rich western peninsula to the bordering lakes, and chiefly to Lake Ontario. The main line was to run in the direction of Governor Simcoe's great highway, Dundas Street, from Burlington Bay to London, while power was taken to extend the road to Lake Huron and the navigable waters of the Thames. Nothing was done under this charter. When it was renewed by an Act of 1845, the name was changed to the Great Western, and, more important, the route was altered to extend from the Niagara river via Hamilton to Windsor and Sarnia. For meanwhile the New York Central had reached Buffalo, and the Michigan Central was being pushed westward from Detroit toward Chicago. A road through Canada would provide a shorter link than one south of Lake Erie, and the Great Western was designed to fill this gap.

With all the possibilities of through and local traffic, and of comparatively good grades and few curves, the road was long in starting. An eminent American engineer, Charles B. Stuart, reported glowingly on the prospects. Two citizens of Hamilton, Allan MacNab, fiery politician and calculating lobbyist, and Isaac Buchanan, untiring advocate of railways, protection, and paper money, threw themselves into the campaign. Samuel Zimmermann, the best known contractor of the period, a Pennsylvanian who had come to Canada to take a Welland Canal contract, and stayed to be the power behind the scenes in the provincial legislature, was prepared to build the road. Hudson gave the scheme his approval. All to no immediate purpose. The contracts were let, ground was broken at London in 1843, but the money to build was not forthcoming. In consequence the Great Western also turned to parliament for aid.

The Toronto, Simcoe and Huron Union Railroad Company—later known as the Northern —the first road in Upper Canada on which steam locomotives were used, was still slower in emerging from the promotion stage. The idea of building a great portage road between Lake Huron and Lake Ontario was an obvious one, and proposals for its construction were frequent. It was not until the scheme was taken up by Frederick Chase Capreol, a sanguine and ingenious Englishman many years resident in Toronto, that any real progress was made. Capreol conceived the brilliant idea of combining the lure of a lottery and the increment of land values to finance a road from Toronto to Georgian Bay. His proposal was to raise funds by a lottery for the purchase of 100,000 acres of land along the route of the railroad, and to pay for the road out of the increase in the value of the land. Objections moral and financial were urged, and Capreol modified his scheme. In 1849 an Act was passed granting a charter and permitting the raising of money either by subscription or by lottery, but it was reserved by the governor-general for royal assent, on account of the lottery clause. Capreol, nothing daunted, sailed for England, and in seven weeks was back with royal assent assured. The lottery, for all its alluring promises, fell flat. Then the Northern, too, clamoured for public aid.

With these local roads under way or actively promoted, still larger projects loomed up. A line from Montreal to Toronto, paralleling the St Lawrence, and thus for the first

Toronto, Simcoe and Huron
RAILROAD UNION COMPANY!

UNION OF INTERESTS!

CAPITAL:—$2,000,000!!

AN EXTENSIVE CANADIAN
RAILROAD UNION TIRAGE!

Founded upon the principle of the Art Unions of England; specially authorised by an Act of the Provincial Parliament; 12th Vic., Cap. 199, and sanctioned by the Royal Assent of Her Majesty in Privy Council, July 30th, 1849,—containing 2,000,000 in stock, in various allotments of

100,000 !—$40,000 !—$20,000—$10,000 ! $5,000—$2,000—1,000—&c.

The proceeds to be applied to construct a Railroad from TORONTO to LAKE HURON, touching at Holland Landing and Barrie. To be PUBLICLY DRAWN at the City Hall, Toronto, under the superintendence of Directors, specially authorised by the Act of Incorporation, consisting the following Gentlemen, viz :

R. C. CAPREOL,	CHARLES BERCZY,
Hon. H. J. BOULTON, M.P.P.	JOSEPH D. RIDOUT,
JOHN HIBBERT,	GEORGE BARROW,
ROBERT EASTON BURNS,	ALBERT FURNISS,
JAS. C. MORRISON, M. P. P.	B. HOLMES, M. P. P.

BANKERS:
The Commercial Bank, M. D., Toronto, and its Various Branches in Canada.

Every Number to be drawn, and each number to have its fate decided in accordance with the plan directed by the Act of Incorporation.

Fourteen days Public Notice to be given previous to day of drawing.

R. C. CAPREOL, MANAGER.
APPOINTED BY THE BOARD OF DIRECTORS.

GRAND PLAN:

2 magnificent allotments of	$100,000 in Stock,		$200,000
6 splendid allotments of	40,000	"	240,000
10 extensive allotments of	20,000	"	200,000
16 large allotments of	10,000	"	160,000
20 allotments of	5,000	"	100,000
50 allotments of	2,000	"	100,000
100 allotments of	1,000	"	100,000
250 allotments of	500	"	125,000
500 allotments of	250	"	125,000
2500 allotments of	100	"	250,000
5000 allotments of	50	"	250,000
7500 allotments of	20	"	150,000
15,954 allotments, amounting to .			**$2,000,000**
100,000 Contributions amount to			**$2,000,000**

Being little more than Five Blanks to an Allotment ! ! !

Contributions $20 each; Halves & Quarters in Proportion.

☞ SCRIP will be issued for allotments, within forty days after the drawing, on payment of twelve per cent, thereon, in compliance with the provisions of the Act of Incorporation.

This Grand and Important Plan is particularly deserving of attention from every class of the community in Canada and various parts of the United States, whether directly interested in Railroads or not. It has been projected as a great public advantage, that of opening a Railway communication across the Peninsula to the Far West, in connection with the lines now finished from New York and Boston to Oswego—thus rendering the Northern Route, by Toronto to the Western States, shorter than any other by several hundred miles—the distance across the Peninsula being only about Eighty Miles, thus avoiding the circuitous and dangerous route by Lake Erie and the Southern shore of Lake Huron.

It is presumed that when this line of Railway is finished, it will be the best paying Stock in North America.

☞ Applications for Tickets (enclosing remittances) to be addressed, post-paid, to

F. C. CAPREOL, *Manager.*

UNION TIRAGE HALL, TORONTO, 1st January, 1850. 495-1

RAILROADS AND LOTTERIES

An Early Canadian Prospectus

time competing with water transport instead of merely supplementing it, began to be talked of as possible. The need of bringing the Maritime Provinces into closer touch with the Canadas lent support to plans of a road from Halifax to Quebec. But for these extensive schemes public aid was even more indispensable.

Hitherto the government of British North America had framed no definite or continuous railway policy. There had been general agreement that railway building should be left to private enterprise. In 1832, when the charter of the Champlain and St Lawrence was under discussion in the legislature of Lower Canada, some members advocated government ownership, but Papineau, the French - Canadian leader, protested against the jobbery that would follow. In the forties the government of Canada was selling its highways to toll-companies, and was not likely to embark on railway construction. In several later charters provision was made for state purchase, after a term of years, at cost plus twenty or twenty-five per cent. Control of private companies in the interest of the shipper was sometimes sought. In the charter of the Champlain and St Lawrence a maximum rate was prescribed at 3d. a mile for passengers and 9¾d. a mile per ton of freight, subject to reduction when profits exceeded twelve per cent. In Upper Canada the earlier charters set no maximum, though the governor in council was given power to approve rates. It appeared to be held that different forwarding companies would make use of the iron way, and afford sufficient competition to protect shippers and passengers against extortion. New Brunswick in 1836 revealed the not modest expectations of profit which prevailed. It provided, in the St Andrews and Quebec charter, that after ten years tolls, if excessive, might be reduced to yield only twenty-five per cent profit. The same sanguine expectations were reflected in the provision made in eight charters issued by Lower Canada between 1845 and 1850, that half the profits over a minimum varying from ten to twenty-four per cent were to go to the state.

The prevalent belief in the great profits to be obtained influenced public opinion against any grant of government aid, except during a brief period before the Rebellion of 1837, when the lavish policy of state construction and state bonuses adopted by the neighbouring republic proved contagious in Upper Canada.

Under the influence of that example the Cobourg Railroad was to be granted a loan of £10,000 as soon as an equal sum was privately subscribed and one-third was paid up. The Toronto and Lake Huron was promised £3 for every £1 of private capital expended, up to £100,000, while the London and Gore was offered a loan of twice that sum; in both these cases the loan was to be secured not only by a lien on the road, but by the liability of the communities benefited to a special tax. None of these generous offers was taken up, and they were not renewed. But a growing realization of the importance of railways and of the evident difficulty of building them in Canada solely by private funds compelled the formation of a new policy of state assistance. This new policy ushered in the first great period of railway construction.

CHAPTER V

THE GRAND TRUNK ERA

IT has been seen that by the close of the
forties British North America was realizing
both the need of railway expansion and the
difficulty of financing it. Other factors combined to bring about the intervention of the
state on a large scale. Both in the Canadas
and in the Maritime Provinces political disputes were giving place to economic activities.
The battle of responsible government had been
fought and won. Men's energies were no
longer absorbed by constitutional strife. Bald-
win and LaFontaine were making way for
Hincks and Morin ; Howe had turned to constructive tasks. Responsibility was bringing
new confidence and new initiative, though
colonial dependence still continued to hamper
enterprise. British and American contractors
discovered the virgin field awaiting them, and
local politicians discovered the cash value of
votes and influence. The example set in the
United States was powerful. Massachusetts

had guaranteed bonds of local roads to the extent of eight millions, without ever having to pay a cent of the interest; and though New York's experience had been more chequered, the successes were stressed and the failures were plausibly explained away.

The eight or ten years which followed 1849 are notable not only for a sudden outburst of railway construction and speculative activity throughout the provinces, but for the beginning of that close connection between politics and railways which is distinctively Canadian. In this era parliament became the field of railway debate. Political motives came to the front: 'statesmen' began to talk of links of Empire and 'politicians' began to press the claims of their constituencies for needed railway communications. Cabinets realized the value of the charters they could grant or the country's credit they could pledge, and contractors swarmed to the feast. 'Railways are my politics,' was the frank avowal of the Conservative leader, Sir Allan MacNab.

Three names are closely linked with this new policy—those of Howe in Nova Scotia, Chandler in New Brunswick, and Hincks in Canada.

Francis Hincks, merchant, journalist, and

politician, moderate reformer, and Canada's first notable finance minister, took the initiative. As inspector-general in the second Baldwin-LaFontaine Cabinet, he brought down the first instalment of his railway policy in 1849. In the previous session a committee of the House had considered the demand of the Great Western and of the St Lawrence and Atlantic for assistance, and had discussed the less advanced proposals for railways from Montreal to Toronto and from Quebec to Halifax. Allan MacNab, as chairman of the committee, had listened sympathetically to the plea of Allan MacNab, president of the Great Western, and the committee had reported in favour of guaranteeing the stock of the two companies to the extent of a million sterling. No action was taken at this session. Meanwhile Hincks, by instruction of his colleagues, had drawn up two memoranda— one suggesting that the crown lands in the province might be offered as security for the capital necessary to build the road within the province, and the other urging the Imperial government to undertake the road from Halifax to Quebec. Capitalists gave no encouragement to the first suggestion, and the British government had not replied to the second by the end of the session of 1848-49. Accordingly, in April 1849 Hincks brought down a new policy, based upon a suggestion of the directors of the St Lawrence and Atlantic. The proposal was, to guarantee the interest, not exceeding six per cent, on half the bonds of any railway over seventy-five miles long, whenever half the road had been constructed, the province to be protected by a first charge after the bondholders' lien. MacNab seconded the resolution; voices from Bytown and the Saguenay mildly questioned the policy, but the resolution passed unanimously.

Even with this aid construction did not proceed apace. It was still necessary for the companies to complete half the road before qualifying for government assistance. This the St Lawrence road effected slowly, in face of quarrels with contractors, repudiation of calls by shareholders, and hesitancy of banks to make advances. The Great Western did not get under way until 1851, when American capitalists, connected with the New York Central, took shares and a place on the directorate. In the same year the Toronto, Simcoe and Huron, later known as the Northern, began construction.

Meanwhile suggestions from the Maritime

Provinces had brought still more ambitious schemes within practical range, and these led Hincks to take the second step in his policy of aid to railways.

In the Maritime Provinces, from 1835 to 1850, many railways had been projected, but, with the exception of a small coal tramway in Nova Scotia, built in 1839 from the Albion coal-mines to tide-water, not a mile was built before 1847. There, as elsewhere, the pamphleteer and the promoter acted as pioneers, and the capitalist and the politician took up their projects later. The plans which chiefly appealed to public attention looked to the linking up of St Andrews, St John, and Halifax with Quebec and Montreal and with the railways of Maine. From the outset the projects in these provinces were much more ambitious than the local beginnings in the Canadas. They were more markedly political and military in aim, and in consequence depended in greater measure upon the aid of the British government. When at last construction was begun, the policy of provincial ownership was more widely adopted.

When in 1876 Sandford Fleming drew up a record of the great work just completed under his direction, the Intercolonial Railway, he called attention to the first proposal for such a road, found in an article contributed to the *United Service Journal* in 1832 by Henry Fairbairn.[1] The author proposed the two chief projects which for half a century were to engross the attention of the Maritime Provinces : a road from St Andrews to Quebec, which should ' convey the whole trade of the St Lawrence, in a single day, to Atlantic waters,' and another line from Halifax through St John to the border of Maine, which should command for Halifax ' the whole stream of passengers, mails, and light articles of commerce passing into the British possessions and to the United States and every part of the continent of America.'

St Andrews was the winter port in British territory nearest to the upper provinces. If the territory in dispute on the Maine boundary fell to New Brunswick and Quebec, a road not more than 250 or 300 miles long could be built from this port to the city of Quebec. In 1835 a Railway Association was formed in St Andrews, an exploratory survey was made, and the interest of Lower Canada was enlisted.

[1] As a matter of fact, discussion of this scheme began in St Andrews in 1827, and in 1828 John Wilson convened a meeting of the citizens to further it.

In the following year New Brunswick gave a charter to the St Andrews and Quebec Railroad, and the Imperial government agreed to bear the cost of a survey. But the survey was speedily halted because of protests from Maine; in 1842 the Ashburton Treaty assigned to the United States a great part of the territory through which the line was projected, and the promoters gave up. Then in 1845 the railway mania in England brought a revival of all colonial schemes. Sir Richard Broun took up the plan for a line from Halifax to Quebec, along with other grandiose projects connected with his endeavour to revive the lost glories of the baronetage of Nova Scotia, but did not get past the stage of forming a provisional committee. This discussion revived the flagging hopes of St Andrews, and, as will be seen in detail later, a beginning was made by a railway from St Andrews to Woodstock, the New Brunswick and Canada, for which ground was broken in November 1847.

The provincial legislature early concluded that it would be impossible to induce private capitalists to build an intercolonial road unaided. They were unanimous also, not yet having emerged from the stage of colonial dependence, in desiring to throw the burden of such aid as far as possible on the British government. In the absence of a colonial federation the United Kingdom was the main connecting-link between the colonies in British North America, and was presumably most interested in matters affecting more than a single colony. The British government, however, had by this time about decided that the old policy of treating the colonies as an estate or plantation of the mother country, protecting or developing them in return for the monopoly of their trade, did not pay. It had reluctantly conceded them political home rule ; it was soon to thrust upon them freedom of trade; and it was not inclined to retain burdens when it had given up privileges. Mr Gladstone, secretary for the Colonies, agreed, however, in 1846, to have a survey made at the expense of the three colonies concerned.

This survey, the starting-point for the controversies and the proposals of a generation, was completed in 1848, under Major Robinson and Lieutenant Henderson of the Royal Engineers. 'Major Robinson's Line,' as it came to be known, ran roughly in the direction eventually followed by the Intercolonial—from Halifax to Truro, and thence north to Miramichi and the Chaleur Bay, and up the

Metapedia valley to the St Lawrence. The distance from Halifax to Quebec was computed at 635 miles, and the cost at £7000 sterling a mile or about £5,000,000. Acting on the assurance of engineers that the route was feasible, each of the three colonial governments offered in 1849 to set aside for the work a belt of crown lands ten miles wide on each side of the railway, and to pledge £20,000 a year to meet interest or expenses, if the British government would undertake the project. Downing Street, however, replied politely but emphatically that no aid could be given.

After the plan of a northern route to Quebec was thus apparently given its quietus, interest shifted to the Portland connections. The building of the road from Montreal to Portland added further strength to the claims of this route. On paper, at least, it seemed possible to make the connection between Montreal and Halifax by following either the northern or the southern sides of the great square. One of the southern sides was now under way, and by building the other, from Portland to St John and Halifax, connection with the Canadas would be completed. Under the leadership once more of John A. Poor, Portland took up the latter project. The name of the proposed road, the European and North American, showed the influence of the same hope which Fairbairn had expressed—that the road from Portland to Halifax would become the channel of communication between the United States and Europe, at least for passengers, mails, and express traffic. With a line of steamers from Halifax to Galway in Ireland, it was held that the journey from New York to London could be cut to six or seven days.

In July 1850 a great convention assembled in Portland, attended by delegates from New Brunswick and Nova Scotia as well as from Maine and other New England states. Intertwined flags and fraternal unity, local development and highways to Europe, prospective profits and ways and means of construction, were the themes of the fervent orators and promoters. The convention was enthusiastically in favour of the project. The 550 miles from Portland to Halifax — 222 in Maine, 204 in New Brunswick, and 124 in Nova Scotia—would cost, it was estimated, $12,000,000, half of which might be raised by private subscription and the rest by state and provincial guarantee.

The delegates from the Maritime Provinces

returned home full of enthusiasm, but increasingly uncertain about the securing of the necessary capital. At this stage Joseph Howe came to the front. He had much earlier, in 1835, before entering parliament, taken the lead in advocating a local railway from Halifax to Windsor, but had not been prominent in recent discussions. He now urged strongly that the province of Nova Scotia should itself construct the section of the European and North American which lay within its borders. He proposed further to seek from the Imperial government a guarantee of the necessary loan, in order that the province might borrow on lower terms. The Colonial Office, while expressing its approval of the Portland scheme, declined to give a guarantee any more than a cash contribution. Nothing daunted, Howe sailed for England in November 1850, and by persistent interviews, eloquent public addresses and exhaustive pamphlets, caught public favour, and in spite of Cabinet changes in London secured the pledge he desired.

In the official reply of the Colonial Office Howe was informed that aid would not be given except for an object of importance to the Empire as a whole, and that accordingly

aid was contingent upon securing help from
New Brunswick and Canada to build the whole
road from Halifax to Quebec. Major Robinson's line need not be followed if a shorter
and better could be secured ; any change,
however, should be subject to the approval
of the British government. 'The British
Government would by no means object to
its forming part of the plan that it should
include provision for establishing a communication between the projected railway and
the railways of the United States.' The
colonies were to bear the whole cost of the
loan, and were to impose taxes sufficient to
provide interest and sinking fund, and thus
ensure against any risk of loss to the United
Kingdom.

Howe returned triumphant. The British
government would guarantee a loan of
£7,000,000, which would build the roads to
Portland and to Quebec and perhaps still
farther west. He hastened to New Brunswick, and won the consent of its government
to the larger plan, went on to Portland and
allayed its murmurs, and with E. B. Chandler
of New Brunswick reached Toronto, then the
seat of government of the province of Canada,
in June 1851. His eloquence and the dazzling

offer of cheap and seemingly unlimited capital soon won consent. The representatives of the three provinces agreed to construct the road from Halifax to Quebec on joint account, while Canada would build the extension from Quebec to Montreal, and New Brunswick the extension to the Maine border, each at its own risk, but in all cases out of the £7,000,000 guaranteed loan.

Then suddenly the bubble burst. The Colonial Office, late in 1851, declared that Howe had been mistaken in declaring that the guarantee was to extend to the European and North American project. The British government had no objection to this road being built, but would not aid it. The officials of the Colonial Office declared that they never meant to promise anything else.

It is difficult to assign with certainty responsibility for this serious misunderstanding. Possibly Howe's optimism and oratorical vagueness led him to misinterpret the promises made, but his reports immediately after the interviews were explicit, and in dispatches and speeches sent to the Colonial Office and acknowledged with high compliments, his version of the agreement had been set forth clearly and for months had gone unchallenged. He cannot be freed from a share of the blame, but the negligence of Downing Street was at least equally the source of the misunderstanding.

The whole plan thus fell to the ground. The consent of the three provinces was essential, and New Brunswick would not support the Halifax and Quebec project if the Portland road, running through the most populous and influential sections of the province, was to be postponed indefinitely. Hincks determined to endeavour to save the situation. Accompanied by John Young and E. P. Taché, he visited Fredericton and Halifax early in 1852, and hammered out a compromise. New Brunswick agreed to join in the Halifax to Quebec project on condition that the road should run from Halifax to St John and thence up the valley of the St John river; Nova Scotia agreed to this change, which made St John rather than Halifax the main ocean terminus, on condition that New Brunswick should bear five-twelfths as against its own three-twelfths of the cost. It remained to secure the consent of the Imperial government to this change in route, and accordingly Hincks, Chandler, and Howe arranged to sail for England early in March. Hincks sailed on the day agreed ; Chandler followed a fortnight later ; Howe, repenting of his bargain, postponed sailing a fortnight, a month, six weeks, and then announced that because of election pressure he could not go at all. Hincks and Chandler found in office in London a new government which appeared biased against the valley route. Upon a peremptory request from Hincks for a definite answer within a fortnight, the British Cabinet, in spite of the previous promise to consider the route an open question, declined to aid any but a road following Major Robinson's line. The negotiations broke off, joint action between the provinces failed, and each province switched to its own separate track.

Howe steadily maintained the policy of state ownership, but had unusual difficulty in carrying Nova Scotia with him. The great English contracting firm of Peto, Brassey, Betts and Jackson, whose operations in the other provinces will be discussed at greater length, offered to find the necessary capital if given the contracts on their own terms. Many Nova Scotians were dazzled by the promises of the agents of this firm, and Howe in 1853 was forced to agree to their proposals. The contractors found themselves unable to make

SIR FRANCIS HINCKS
From a portrait in the Dominion Archives

good their promises, in face of panics on the stock market in England, and in the following year Howe's original policy was sanctioned. He himself retired from political life for a time in order to carry through, as one of the railway commissioners, the policy he had steadfastly urged.

It was on June 13, 1854, that the first sod was turned for the construction of the Nova Scotia Railway, and a beginning made at last. The road was to run from Halifax to Truro, with a branch to Windsor. Progress was slow, but by 1858 the ninety-three miles planned had been completed. Then came a halt, when reality succeeded the glowing visions of the prospectus, the service proved poor, and the returns low. Nine years later an extension from Truro to Pictou was constructed. This gave Nova Scotia at Confederation in 1867 145 miles of railroad in all, built at a cost of $44,000 a mile, and connecting Halifax with the Bay of Fundy and the Gulf of St Lawrence. The gauge adopted was five feet six, and the Nova Scotia road led the way in Canada in using coal for fuel.

New Brunswick had a more chequered experience. After the collapse of the Halifax and Quebec project, her efforts were confined to the road running north from St Andrews and to the European and North American.

The possibilities of St Andrews as an ocean terminus had been severely hampered by the thrusting in of the Maine-wedge between New Brunswick and Quebec, but still the town struggled on. In 1847 shares in the railway had been placed both in England and in the province, and the legislature guaranteed the interest on debentures and also granted a land subsidy. Still, the money came in slowly. Operations were time and again suspended, contract after contract was made, and re-organizations were effected. In 1858 the road had reached Canterbury, and four years later its temporary terminus at Richmond; in 1866 a branch to St Stephen was opened, and in 1868 an extension to Woodstock, making 126 miles all told, costing about $20,000 a mile. At Confederation only a third of the distance between St Andrews and Rivière du Loup on the St Lawrence had been completed, and the road was in a receiver's hands.

The European and North American also had its troubles. Maine proved unable to build its section. In 1852 the New Brunswick government made a contract with the English firm already referred to, under the style of Peto, Betts, Jackson and Brassey, for the construction of a line from Maine to Nova Scotia, at $32,500 a mile. The province agreed to subscribe $6000 stock and lend $9400 in bonds per mile ; the contractors were to find the rest of the money in England. This they failed to do. The firm was dissolved in 1856, and the government took over the road, completing it from St John to Shediac, 108 miles, in 1860. The western half was not begun until August 1867.

To return to the upper provinces. By 1851 the St Lawrence, the Great Western, and the Northern were under way, and more ambitious schemes proposed. The Guarantee Act of 1849, which was the first phase of Hincks's policy, assuring public aid for the second half of any road at least seventy-five miles in length, was proving inadequate, and the government was considering an extension of its policy. At this juncture the golden news arrived of Howe's success in securing the £7,000,000 loan at bargain rates. All hesitation was removed. No doubt was felt that the roads would pay, once they were built ; the only difficulty had been to find the money to build them. And now £7,000,000 was available—£4,000,000 of it for Canada, at probably 3½ per cent. Paper computations soon proved that £4,000,000 would suffice not only to build Canada's third of the Quebec-Halifax route, but to build a trunk line from Quebec or Montreal through to Hamilton, whence the Great Western ran to Windsor on the frontier opposite Detroit.

At once a struggle began for the control of this fund. The Montreal merchants who had bought experience in building the St Lawrence and Atlantic, John Young, Luther Holton, and D. L. Macpherson, with A. T. Galt of Sherbrooke, were first in the field, and pressed for a charter to build from Montreal to Kingston, intending later to extend this road to Toronto. Then the most noted firm of contractors in railway history, Peto, Brassey, Betts and Jackson (the forms of the firm name varied), who had built one-third of the railways of Britain, and also roads in France and Spain and Italy and Prussia and India, were attracted to this fresh field by Howe's campaign in England. They sent an agent to Toronto in 1851 to offer to construct all the roads needed, and to find all the capital required, with partial government guarantees.

Hincks, with whom the decision lay, was

eminently an opportunist. In 1849 he had
argued against government ownership; now he
argued for it. Yet he did not close the door
against retreat. The new Act, passed in April
1852, marked the second or Grand Trunk phase
of his gradually shaping policy. Besides providing for the Canadian share of the Halifax
to Quebec road, the Act contemplated three
alternative methods of continuing this Trunk
line westward. The province was to build it
if the guaranteed loan could be stretched far
enough; failing this, the province, together
with such municipalities as wished, could
undertake the extension; should both modes
fail, private companies might be given the
privilege, with a provincial guarantee of half
the cost, covering both principal and interest.
No roads except those forming part of the
Trunk line and the three already under way
were to be aided. The Montreal and Kingston Railway, in which Holton, Galt, and Macpherson were prime movers, was chartered,
and also the Kingston and Toronto, but in
both charters a suspending clause was included
preventing the charters from taking effect
until special proclamation was made—after
the other plans had failed.

The next move was to arrange terms with

the other provinces and secure the promised Imperial guarantee. How Hincks and Chandler's mission failed has already been told. Hincks then made another sharp curve and decided for company control. Before leaving Canada he had made up his mind that the construction should be entrusted to British contractors, and was authorized to negotiate with the Brassey firm. Now that the Imperial guarantee had faded away, capital was needed more than contractors. The Brasseys promised both, offering, if given the contract, to organize a company in England which would provide all the capital not guaranteed by the province.

This seductive offer was to prove the main cause of the financial embarrassment of the Grand Trunk. It involved at the outset a dubious connection between company and contractor, and also for two generations an attempt to manage a great railway at a range of three thousand miles. So fatal did it prove that in later years each party to it endeavoured to throw the responsibility for the initiative on the other, and enemies of Hincks declared that he, as well as Lord Elgin, the governor-general, had been bribed to wreck the negotiations with the British government in order to take up with Brassey. Whether or not Hincks was first to resume negotiations in London, it was the contractors who had already taken the initiative in America, sending a representative to Toronto, and taking part in the elections of 1851 in Nova Scotia against Howe. It is clear also that the British government was unwilling to consider anything but the unacceptable Major Robinson line. Hincks was justified in looking elsewhere for capital, but he was not justified in binding himself to one firm of contractors, however eminent.

Hincks returned to Canada with a tentative contract in his pocket. To Canada, too, came Henry Jackson, a partner in the Brassey firm for this enterprise, and one of the most skilful and domineering of the railway lobbyists in Canada's annals, rich in such methods. At once a battle royal began in parliament. On August 7, 1852, the Montreal and Kingston and the Kingston and Toronto charters were proclaimed in force ; apparently the supposition of the government was that the English contractors would simply subscribe for the bulk of the stock in these companies. But the Canadian promoters were not willing to give up their rights so easily : a week after the books were opened, Galt, Holton, and Macpherson subscribed between them £596,500 and seven of their associates took up the nominal balance of the capital of £600,000 which was authorized. Hincks met this move by bringing down a bill to incorporate a new company, the Grand Trunk Railway Company of Canada, and the rights of the rival claimants came before parliament for decision.

On behalf of the English promoters it was urged that the Canadian promoters could not raise the necessary capital, that the Galt-Holton-Macpherson subscription was a fake, that the English contractors could induce capitalists to invest freely at low rates, and that their superior methods would result in a road of more solid construction and lower working expenses than the ordinary American railway. Holton and Galt, on the other hand, contended that their subscription was in good faith, that tenders were in, and that with provincial guarantee and municipal aid, and by paying the contractors partly in stock, they could finance the road. It would be better, they urged, to have the control in the hands of men who knew the province rather than in the hands of outsiders. The Grand Trunk Company, seeking incorporation, was only a sham company, under the thumb of the contractors, formed to ratify a foregone contract with them. If the Montreal and Kingston Company was given control, it would invite the Brassey firm to tender on the same basis as other contractors : no more could honestly be asked.

Galt and Holton had the best of the argument, but Hincks had the votes, and rumours which Jackson spread of the Brassey millions and the firm's open door to all the money markets of Europe brought conviction or afforded excuse. The railway committee reported in favour of the English promoters, though the competition had compelled them to reduce their price by a thousand pounds a mile, and to accept a guarantee of £3000 per mile instead of half the cost. At the same time the Brassey firm secured a charter for the Grand Trunk of Canada East, to run from Quebec to Trois Pistoles—Canada's first section of the Halifax to Quebec route. The same aggressive firm had already secured a contract for the Quebec and Richmond, which was to join the St Lawrence and Atlantic at Richmond, and, as has been seen, for New Brunswick and Nova Scotia roads. With these contracts seemingly secure, Jackson sailed for home. But Canadian promoters were quick to learn. Galt had another card to play. As president of the St Lawrence and Atlantic he proposed to amalgamate this road with the Montreal and Kingston, and to build a bridge at Montreal, thus securing an essential part of the trunk line. Hincks became alarmed at the Montreal interests thus arrayed against him, and proposed as a compromise that the Grand Trunk should absorb the St Lawrence road and build the bridge at Montreal on the condition that the opposition to its westward plans should be abandoned. Upon this all parties agreed, and the English and Canadian promoters joined forces.

Negotiations were completed in England early in 1853. As yet the Grand Trunk Company was but a name. The real parties to the bargain were many. First came John Ross, a member of the Canadian Cabinet, but representing the future Grand Trunk, of which he was elected president. The Barings and Glyns, eminent banking houses, had a twofold part to play, as they were closely connected with the contractors and were also the London agents of the Canadian government. The contractors themselves, Peto, Brassey, Betts and Jackson, of whom Jackson, accompanied by the company's engineer, A. M. Ross, had spent a year studying the Canadian situation, put in anxious weeks hammering out the details of the agreement and the prospectus to follow it. Galt represented the St Lawrence and Atlantic and the Atlantic and St Lawrence, while Rhodes and Forsythe of Quebec had charge of the interests of the Quebec and Richmond. An agreement was reached to amalgamate all the Canadian roads and to lease the Maine road for 999 years. This left Toronto the western terminus. An attempt to absorb the Great Western and thus secure an extension to Windsor came to nothing. This failure gave Galt an opening for another brilliant stroke of railway strategy. A company had recently been chartered to build a road from Toronto to Guelph and Sarnia, and the firm of Gzowski and Co., of which Galt was a member, had secured the contract. Galt, acting with Alexander Gillespie, a prominent London financier who was the agent of the Toronto, Guelph and Sarnia Railway, now proposed to substitute this line as the westward extension. Everybody was in an amalgamating mood, and the bargain went through. All contracts previously made were taken over by the amalgamated company, and the investing public was told that all uncertainty as to the total amount was thus removed—as it emphatically was, for the time.

A glowing prospectus was drawn up. The amalgamated road would be the most comprehensive railway system in the world, comprising 1112 miles, stretching from Portland and eventually from Halifax (by both the northern and the southern route) to Lake Huron. The whole future traffic between west and east must therefore pass over the Grand Trunk, as both geographical conditions and legislative enactment prevented it from injurious competition. 'Commencing at the debouchere [*sic*] of the three longest lakes in the world,' the prospectus continued, ' it pours the accumulating traffic in one unbroken line throughout the entire length of Canada into the St Lawrence at Montreal and Quebec, on which it rests on the north, while on the south it reaches the magnificent harbours of Portland and St John on the ocean.' It was backed by government guarantee and Canadian investment, and its execution was in the hands of the most eminent contractors. The total capital was fixed at £9,500,000 sterling. The revenue was estimated at nearly £1,500,000 a year, which, with working expenses at *forty* per cent of revenue, and debenture interest and £60,000 for lease of the Atlantic and St Lawrence Railway deducted, would leave £550,000 or 11½ per cent on the share capital.

On the advice of Baring and Glyn only half the capital was issued at first. This decision proved a serious mistake. In 1853, when the company was floated, money was abundant and cheap ; the shares and bonds issued were over-subscribed twenty times, and were quoted at a premium before allotment. Scarcely was the issue made when war with Russia loomed up, and money rose from three to seven or eight per cent. Never again was it possible for the Grand Trunk to secure capital in such abundance.

But this was for the future to disclose. At once construction began in Canada. A. M. Ross was appointed chief engineer, and S. P. Bidder general manager, both on the nomination of the English bankers and contractors. Plant was assembled in Canada, orders for rails and equipment were placed in England, and navvies came out by the thousand. At one time 14,000 men were directly employed upon the railways in Upper Canada alone. In July 1853 the last gaps in the St Lawrence and Atlantic had been filled up, though not in permanent fashion. In 1854 the Quebec and Richmond section was opened; in 1855, the road from Montreal to Brockville and from Lévis to St Thomas, Quebec; in 1856, the Brockville to Toronto and Toronto to Stratford sections. Not until 1858 was the western road completed as far as London. The year 1859 saw the completion of the Victoria Bridge, the extension from St Mary's to Sarnia, and a new road in Michigan, running from Port Huron to Detroit. By 1860 the eastern section extended to Rivière du Loup, where a halt was made.

From the outset difficulties undreamed of had developed. Money was hard to get and early traffic returns were disappointing, so that the company found it almost impossible to secure the balance of the capital required. The road from Montreal to Portland was found to require heavy expenditure to bring it up to the standard. The contractors, for their part, were embarrassed by the company's shortage of funds and by the great rise in the prices of land, materials, and labour. Their own activities, the Reciprocity Treaty of 1854 with the United States, the Crimean War, had combined to bring on a period of inflated prices such as Canada was not to experience again for half a century. With wheat at two dollars a bushel, and ' land selling by the inch,' even liberal margins of profit on contracts vanished.[1]

In these straits the company turned to the government for aid. It had many supporters in the House. No one could deny the benefits which its operations had conferred upon the province. The government guarantee of interest and the government nomination of a part of the board of directors were plausibly held to involve responsibility for the solvency of the company. It was not surprising, therefore, that for a decade after 1855 scarcely a year passed without a bill to amend the terms

[1] The Brassey firm were paid about £9000 sterling a mile for the line from Toronto to Montreal, £8000 for the section from Quebec to Rivière du Loup, £6500 for the Quebec and Richmond road, and £1,400,000 for the Victoria Bridge. Gzowski and Co., consisting of Messrs Gzowski, Holton, Macpherson, and Galt, secured the Toronto to Sarnia contract at £8000 a mile. In both cases these prices included equipment. The English contractors were required to take a large portion of their pay in depreciated bonds and stock, whereas the Canadian contractors were given cash; on the other hand, Brassey had a higher price and less difficult country to work in. The English firm, with all their experience, were not familiar with building roads in countries where labour was dear, and the plant they sent out was antiquated compared with the labour-saving equipment familiar to American and Canadian contractors. They claimed to have lost a million pounds on their enterprise, while Galt, Holton, Macpherson, and Gzowski all made fortunes.

of the Grand Trunk agreement. One year it was an additional guarantee, another a temporary loan, again a postponement, and again a still further postponement of the government's lien. It soon came to be recognized that the money which had been advanced under the guarantee provisions must be considered a gift, not a loan, though to this day the amount nominally due still figures as an asset on the Dominion government's books. Incidentally, the embarrassing government directors were dispensed with in 1857.

The Grand Trunk was complete from Lake Huron to the Atlantic in 1860. In the ten years that followed, working expenses varied from fifty-eight to eighty-five per cent of the gross receipts, instead of the forty per cent which the prospectus had foreshadowed ; not a cent of dividend was paid on ordinary shares—nor has been to this day.

What were the reasons for this disappointing result ? The root of the trouble was that the road was not built solely or even mainly with a view to operating efficiency and earning power. It was the politicians' road, the promoters' road, the contractors' road, at least as much as the shareholders' road. The government had encouraged the building of unprofitable sections, such as that east of Quebec, for local or patriotic reasons. Promoters had unloaded the Portland road and later the Detroit and Port Huron road at excessive prices. The contractors, east of Toronto, had had an eye mainly to construction profits in planning the route, and heavy grades, bad rails, and poor ballast increased maintenance charges beyond all expectations. The prophecy that operating expenses would not exceed forty per cent of earnings, based on English experience, failed partly because earnings were lower, but more because operating expenses were higher, than anticipated. The company had more than its share of hard luck from commercial depression, and from loss on American paper money in the Civil War. Water competition proved serious in the east, while other railways waged traffic wars in Upper Canada. The trade of the far west, which had been the most attractive lure, did not come in any great amount for the first twenty years. Differences of gauge, lack of permanent connections at Chicago, lack of return freight, rate wars with the American roads which had been built west at the same time or later, the inferiority of Montreal to New York as of old in harbour facilities and ocean service, the failure of Portland to become a great commercial centre—all meant hope and dividends deferred. Finally, the management was working at long range: the road did not enjoy the vigilant inspection or the public support that would have attended control by Canadian interests.

The Grand Trunk did Canada good service, well worth all the public aid that was given. It would probably have given better service, and its shareholders could not have fared worse, had the plans of Galt and his associates not been interfered with, and the line been built gradually under local control.

While the building of the Grand Trunk was the main achievement of the period, it was by no means the only one. The fifties were the busiest years in the railway annals of older Canada. In 1850 there were only 66 miles of road in all the provinces. In 1860 there were 2065, of which over 1700 had been added in the Canadas alone. The Great Western and the Northern were pushed forward under the provisions of the earlier Guarantee Act; roads of more local interest were fostered by municipal rivalry. Their building brought unwonted activity in every branch of commerce. A speculative fever ran through the whole community; fortunes were made and lost in the provision trade, and land prices soared to heights undreamed of. This mood was the promoter's happy chance, and still more charters were sought. The pace quickened till exhaustion, contagious American panics, poor harvests, and the Crimean War —which first raised the price of the wheat Canada had to sell, but later raised the price of the money she had to borrow—brought collapse in 1857.

In this boom period jobbery and lobbying reigned to an extent which we rarely realize in our memory of the good old times. Railway contractors were all-powerful in the legislature, and levied toll at will. The most notable 'contractor-boss' of the day was able, dealing with the Great Western, to hold up a bill for double-tracking until assured of the contract himself; dealing with the Grand Trunk, to force from the English contractors a share in the enterprise before consenting to help their schemes through; with the Northern, to collect $100,000 as a condition of securing from the government the guarantee bonds before they had been rightly earned. Municipal officials were bribed to help bonuses through.   Existing roads were blackmailed by pedlars of rival charters. Glaringly fraudulent prospectuses were issued. On a smaller scale, the excitement and the rascality which had marked the beginning of the great railway eras in the United Kingdom and the United States were reproduced in Canada.

Of the other roads completed in this period, the two which had been aided by Hincks's first Guarantee Act were most important.

The Great Western had a promising outlook. It ran through a rich country and had assured prospects of through western traffic. The road was completed from Suspension Bridge to Windsor in January 1854. An extension from Hamilton to Toronto was built in 1856, and a semi-independent line from Galt to Guelph absorbed in 1860. The Great Western came nearest of any early road to being a financial success ; alone of the guaranteed roads it repaid the government loan, nearly in full. But after a brief burst of prosperity, from 1854 to 1856, it, too, was continually in difficulties. In 1856 it paid a dividend of $8\frac{1}{2}$ per cent, but three years later it paid nothing, and in the next decade averaged less than three per cent.

The troubles of the Great Western came

chiefly from competition, actual and threatened, and uncertain traffic connections. To the north, the chartering of the Toronto, Guelph and Sarnia, amalgamated later with the Grand Trunk, cut into its best territory. An endeavour was made in 1854 to divide the remaining area, but two years later the battle was renewed, the Great Western building to Sarnia and the Grand Trunk tapping London and Detroit. Between the Great Western and Lake Erie a rival road direct from Buffalo to Detroit was threatened time and again, but was not built until after Confederation. South of Lake Erie the Lake Shore and Michigan Southern was built shortly afterwards by interests connected with the New York Central, thus threatening the traffic connections of the Great Western both east and west. To avert loss of its western trade, the Great Western sunk large sums in aiding the construction of a road from Detroit to Grand Haven, with ferry connections to Milwaukee ; but this experiment did not prove a success and caused serious embarrassment.

The Northern Railway, whose promoters, as we have seen, naïvely recognized that railways and lotteries were close akin, was opened as far as Allandale in 1853, and to Collingwood in 1855. It was scamped by the contractors, poorly built, and overloaded with debt. The sanguine policy of building up a through traffic from the American West, by water to Collingwood and rail to Toronto, proved a will-o'-the-wisp. In turn the company relied on independent steamers, and set up a fleet of its own, but equally in vain so far as profit went. By 1859 the road was bankrupt. A new general manager, Frederick Cumberland, brought in a change of policy. Local traffic was sedulously cultivated, and a fair degree of prosperity followed.

Most of the lesser roads constructed looked to the municipalities rather than to the provinces for aid. The Municipal Loan Fund of 1854 was the third and last phase of Hincks's railway policy. This was an ingenious attempt to give the municipalities the prestige of provincial connection without accepting any legal responsibility. Municipalities had previously been permitted to bonus or take stock in railways and toll-roads, but their securities were unknown in the world's markets. Hincks now provided that municipalities which wished money to aid railways or other local improvements might practically pool their credit and share in the credit of the province. Provincial debentures were issued against the municipal obligations pooled in the Fund, and the proceeds of their sale given to the municipalities. A sinking fund was to be maintained, and, if need be, the province could levy through the sheriff on any defaulting town.

The municipalities made full use of their privileges. It was believed that railway investments would yield high dividends, and the more optimistic expected to see all taxes made unnecessary by the profits earned. Town vied with town in extravagant enterprises.[1] Not a cent brought a dividend; instead, the municipalities found themselves saddled with heavy interest payments. One after another declined to pay; Port Hope was $312,000 in arrears by 1861 and Cobourg $313,000. The provincial government had

[1] Port Hope borrowed for railway investment $740,000, Cobourg and Brantford $500,000 each, and Brockville $400,000 —all towns of less than 5000 people. The counties of Lanark and Renfrew borrowed $800,000, and villages borrowed in proportion. In all some $6,500,000 was borrowed through the Loan Fund for railway purposes alone, the bulk of it in Upper Canada, while another three million was invested by towns that borrowed on their own responsibility. To aid the Brockville and Ottawa Railway, for example, Lanark and Renfrew advanced $800,000, Brockville $415,000, and the township of Elizabethtown $150,000, or over half the cost of the road. Huron and Bruce invested $300,000 in the Buffalo and Lake Huron, and other municipalities $578,000, and so on throughout the province.

not the political courage to send in the sheriff, and accordingly it was forced at last to assume the whole burden. Prudent municipalities which had declined to borrow at eight per cent found themselves compelled to share the burdens of their reckless neighbours. Demoralization was widespread.

The railways constructed by such aid may be briefly noted. The Buffalo and Lake Huron, extending from Fort Erie to Goderich, was completed in 1858. It had its origin in the ambition of Buffalo to have more immediate connection with the rich western peninsula of Upper Canada and the Lake trade beyond than was afforded by the Great Western. The London and Port Stanley, built in 1854-56, mainly by the city of London, with smaller contributions from Middlesex and Elgin counties and the city of St Thomas, failed to realize the expectations that it would become the main artery of trade between Canada and the states across the lake, but it developed a fair excursion trade and coal traffic, and indirectly justified its construction. The Erie and Ontario portage road, rebuilt in 1854, has already been noted. Another portage road round Niagara Falls was the Welland Railway, planned by W. Hamilton Merritt, the projector of the Welland Canal. It ran from Port Colborne on Lake Erie to Port Dalhousie on Lake Ontario, twenty-five miles, and was completed in 1859, only to add one more to the list of unprofitable roads, and eventually to be absorbed by the Great Western.

Farther east the rivalry of Port Hope and Cobourg led to the construction of two roads, the Cobourg and Peterborough and the Port Hope, Lindsay and Beaverton. Both relied chiefly on timber traffic and aimed to develop the farming country in the rear. The Cobourg line, begun in 1853, suffered disaster from the start : the contractor's extras absorbed all the cash available ; the three-mile bridge built on piles across Rice Lake gave way, and after $1,000,000 had been expended the road was sold for $100,000. The Port Hope line, which absorbed a branch from Millbrook to Peterborough in 1867, fared somewhat better. The Brockville and Ottawa was a lumber road, carrying supplies up and timber down. It was chartered to run from Brockville to Pembroke, with a branch from Smith's Falls on the Rideau Canal to Perth. By 1859 it had reached Almonte, and six years later struggled as far as Sand Point on the Ottawa, when it

halted, till the Canadian Pacific project gave
it new life.   After failing to make ends meet
for some years the company went through
repeated reorganizations in the early sixties.
The Bytown and Prescott, later the St Lawrence and Ottawa, built in 1854, was also a
lumber road, promoted by interests connected
with the Ogdensburg Railway, whose terminus
was opposite Prescott.   It suffered the same
financial fate, and was sold to the English
company which had supplied the rails, at a
total sacrifice of municipal and other creditors'
interests.   Around the Long Sault rapids in
the Ottawa there was built in 1854 the thirteen-
mile Carillon and Grenville, a summer portage
road, an early enterprise which retained its
independence and its old five-foot-six-inch
gauge until 1912, when it was absorbed by the
Canadian Northern.   In Lower Canada the
only minor road built which has not been
referred to was the Stanstead, Shefford and
Chambly, opened in 1859 from St Johns to
Granby, and forming practically an extension
of the Champlain and St Lawrence from the
former point.

CHAPTER VI

THE INTERCOLONIAL

THE first ' age of iron—and of brass ' came to an end before 1860. Between 1850 and 1860, it has been seen, the mileage of all the provinces grew from 66 to 2065. By 1867 it had increased only 213 miles. In two of the intervening years not a mile was built. A halt had come, for stock-taking and heart-searching.

This first era of activity had given as its most obvious result over two thousand miles of railway. In Nova Scotia, Halifax was linked with the Bay of Fundy and the Gulf of St Lawrence ; in New Brunswick, St John was connected with the Gulf, and a road was struggling Canadaward from St Andrews. In the Canadas a ' Grant Trunk,' so nicknamed, ran from Rivière du Loup the whole length of the province to Sarnia, while lesser roads opened up new districts to the north or gave connection with the grain-fields and the ocean ports of the United States. The western province, at all events, was well served for a pioneer country, and the shipper and consumer had no great cause for complaint.

To the taxpayer it seemed otherwise. He had been induced to embark on a lavish policy of financial aid on the assurance that the roads would at worst be no burden, and at best might yield large profits to the state. As a matter of fact, nine out of every ten dollars advanced might be written off as lost. The Grand Trunk, Great Western, and Northern roads were indebted to the old province of Canada on July 1, 1867, in over twenty million dollars for principal advanced and in over thirteen millions for interest. Other roads were indebted to Canadian municipalities in nearly ten millions for principal alone. Yet the taxpayer was not wholly justified in his grumbling. There had been waste and mismanagement, it is true, but the railways had brought indirect gain that more than offset the direct loss. Farming districts were opened up rapidly, freights were reduced in many sections, intercourse was facilitated, and land values were raised. The contribution to the railways was bread well cast upon the waters. It would have been better, if foresight had equalled hindsight, to have given the money out and out.

For the shareholder, English or Canadian, there was little but disappointment. Grand Trunk ordinary stock in 1865 was selling at 22, and even Great Western at 65. The securities of several of the minor roads had been almost entirely wiped out by reorganizations. In 1866 some $4,180,000 was paid in dividends and leases, representing only 2·7 per cent on the $158,000,000 which the roads had cost or were alleged to have cost. Premature extension into unremunerative territory, for political or contracting reasons, excessive competition in the fertile areas, heavy fixed charges on inflated capital or leased roads, water competition, absentee proprietorship, all played their part. Whatever the causes, the results were clear, and capitalists long fought shy of Canadian railway projects.

In the first thirty years of Canadian railway development no question aroused more interest than that of the gauge to be adopted. The cows of the good Dutch burghers of New Amsterdam fixed the windings of Broadway as they remain to this day. The width of the carts used in English coal-mines centuries ago still determines the gauge of railway track and railway cars over nearly all the world. ' Before every engine,' declares Mr H. G. Wells, ' trots the ghost of a superseded horse.' When the steam locomotive was invented, and used upon the coal-mine tramways, it was made of the same four-foot-eight-and-a-half-inch gauge. In England, in spite of the pre-ferences of Brunel, Stephenson's great rival, for a seven-foot gauge, the narrower width soon triumphed, though the Great Western did not entirely abandon its wider track until 1892. In Canada the struggle was longer and more complicated.

It was a question on which engineers differed. Speed, steadiness, cost of track construction, and cost of maintenance were all to be con-sidered, and were all diversely estimated. In early years, before the need of standard-izing equipment was felt, many experiments were made, especially in the United States. In the southern states five feet was the usual width, and the Erie was built on a gauge of six feet, to fit an engine bought at a bar-gain. But in the United States, as in England, the four-foot-eight-and-a-half-inch width was dominant, and would have been adopted in Canada without question, had not local interests, appealing, as often, to patriotic prejudice, succeeded in clouding the issue.

When the road from Portland to Montreal was being planned, the astute Portland promoters insisted upon a gauge of five feet six inches, to prevent the switching of traffic to Boston. Montreal, in its turn, insisted on the same gauge for the Grand Trunk line, to ensure that all east-bound traffic should be brought through Canada to Montreal. It carried its point, and the wider or ' provincial ' gauge became the standard in the Canadas, and later in the Maritime Provinces.

Experience proved that it was impossible to maintain different gauges in countries so closely connected as Canada and the United States. As roads became consolidated into larger systems, the inconvenience of transhipping at break of gauge became more intolerable. The expedients of lifting cars bodily to other trucks, of making axles adjustable, and even of laying a third rail, proved unsatisfactory. Late in the sixties and early in the seventies the Great Western and the Grand Trunk had to adopt the four-foot-eight-and-a-half-inch gauge solely, and other lines gradually followed.

Meanwhile, the cry was going up for a still

narrower gauge. In pioneer districts, at least, it was contended, a road three feet six inches wide, such as had recently been adopted in Norway, would suffice, and would be much cheaper both to build and to operate. Between 1868 and 1873 two experimental narrow-gauge lines were built running north from Toronto—the Toronto and Nipissing, and the Toronto, Grey and Bruce. This proved only a temporary diversion, however, and the decision of the Dominion government in 1874 to change the gauge of the Intercolonial to four feet eight and a half inches, and the adoption of the same standard by the Ontario government, ended the controversy.

Memory is short and hope eternal. Soon after Confederation another burst of activity began in all the provinces of the new Dominion. It was distinctly the period of local development.

In Ontario the opportunity which the fertile western peninsula, jutting down between New York and Michigan, offered for both local and through traffic, led to many projects, much parliamentary jockeying, and at last construction. The Canada Southern was built in 1873, running between Fort Erie, opposite

Buffalo, and Amherstburg on the Detroit river. It was controlled by the Vanderbilt interests and operated in close co-operation with their other roads, the Michigan Southern, Michigan Central, and New York Central. The Great Western met this attack upon its preserves by building in the same year the Canada Air Line, from Glencoe near St Thomas, to Fort Erie, giving more direct connection with Buffalo. Both roads made use of the magnificent International Bridge, built across the Niagara in 1873, under Grand Trunk control.

The marked feature of this period, so far as Ontario was concerned, was the rivalry of the cities along the lake and river front in building new roads to tap the north country. From London there was built in 1875 the London, Huron and Bruce, halting at Wingham. From Hamilton, or rather from Guelph, with connections to Hamilton, the Wellington, Grey and Bruce reached Southampton on Lake Huron in 1873 and Kincardine in 1874. Both roads were virtually branches of the Great Western, and were expected to bring to London and to Hamilton respectively the trade of the rich northwestern counties. The Ambitious City, as Hamilton came to be called at this period, a few years later invaded the Northern Railway's territory by a line from Hamilton to Collingwood, also extended southerly to Port Dover, but control of this road was immediately acquired by the Northern interests. From still more ambitious Toronto two narrow-gauge routes were built between 1869 and 1874—the Toronto, Grey and Bruce running northwest to Owen Sound and Teeswater, and the Toronto and Nipissing northeast to Coboconk and Sutton. Whitby also had its visions of terminal greatness, when the Whitby and Port Perry was built in the later seventies. The Port Hope, Beaverton and Lindsay, renamed the Midland, was pushed northeast to Orillia in 1872 and to Midland in 1875. Cobourg's unfortunate northern line was continued to the iron mines of Marmora. Belleville was linked with Peterborough in 1878-79 by the Grand Junction. Kingston, with the co-operation of interests in New York state, planned the Kingston and Pembroke, which reached Mississippi in 1878, and five years later compromised on Renfrew as a terminus. The bankruptcy of the Brockville and Ottawa did not prevent its extension through an allied company, the Canada Central, to Pembroke in 1869 and to

Ottawa, by a branch from Carleton Place, in 1876.

In Quebec the chief developments were the building of a line connecting Quebec, Montreal, and Ottawa along the north shore of the St Lawrence, and of further connections between Montreal and Quebec and United States roads. The North Shore route had been projected early in the fifties, but, in spite of lavish cash and land bonuses, it was not until the Quebec government took it up as a provincial road, in the seventies, that it was pushed to completion. On the south shore the Eastern Townships triangle was interlaced by a series of smaller roads. From Lévis, opposite Quebec, the Lévis and Kennebec ran south to the Maine border, and the Quebec Central to Sherbrooke. From Sherbrooke and Lennoxville the Massawappi Valley gave connection with the Connecticut and Passumpsic, to which it was leased for 999 years, while branches of the Central Vermont and minor roads opened up new sections and gave further connection with Montreal.

An interesting experiment, motived by the same desire for cheap pioneer construction which in Ontario brought in the narrow gauge, was the wooden railway built in 1870 from

Quebec to Gosford. The rails were simply strips of seasoned maple, $14' \times 7'' \times 4''$, notched into the sleepers and wedged in without the use of a single iron spike. The engine and car wheels were made wide to fit the rail. In spite of its cheap construction the road did not pay, and the hope of extending it as far as Lake St John was deferred for a generation. A similar wooden railway was built from Drummondville to L'Avenir.

In Nova Scotia the chief local development was the opening in 1869 of a road through the Annapolis Valley, the Windsor and Annapolis. This formed an extension of the government road from Halifax to Windsor, but the province preferred to entrust it to a private company, giving a liberal bonus. In New Brunswick there was much activity, all by private companies. The western section of the European and North American, from St John to the Maine boundary, was completed in 1869, though it was not until 1871 that the road was opened through to Portland—by a more circuitous route than Poor had originally planned. From Fredericton a branch was built to meet this road, and a line to Woodstock, which in turn was connected with the old New Brunswick and Canada, still

pushing slowly north. In the meantime Prince
Edward Island was building a narrow-gauge
railway nearly two hundred miles long; in
1873 she was forced into Confederation to find
aid in paying for it.

All this varied activity was made possible by
a revival of the policy of provincial and municipal assistance. Whether from reasoned conviction as to the indirect benefits of more
roads, or because of the log-rolling activities
of rival towns and wily promoters, a systematic and generous policy of aid was adopted.
This aid came chiefly from the provinces and
municipalities, the Dominion as yet confining
itself to works of inter-provincial concern.
Outright gifts for the most part took the place
of loans, since experience had proved that
direct returns upon the money invested were
not to be looked for. Curiously meandering
were the routes which promoters mapped out
in the endeavour to follow the shortest line
between two bonuses.[1]

[1] Ontario in 1871 offered subsidies ranging from two to four
thousand dollars a mile for colonization roads to the north;
Quebec in 1869 offered money and later land; New Brunswick
in 1864 gave $10,000 a mile to various roads, besides taking
$300,000 in stock in the European; while Nova Scotia aided the
Annapolis extension. Municipal aid was even more lavish in
proportion: Toronto gave $350,000 to the Toronto, Grey and

Governments could help to build roads, but could not ensure for them traffic. It took very few years to show that the interests of the public were not best served by scores of petty isolated roads, and that the interests of shareholders were not secured by the cut-throat competition which prevailed in certain areas. This competition was keenest between the roads which were intimately connected with the lines in the United States and dependent upon through traffic. The Grand Trunk had cut into the territory of the Great Western by acquiring the Buffalo and Lake Huron line, and the Canada Southern and the Great Western were disputing for every ton of freight between the Niagara and the Detroit. All were involved in the rate wars which marked this period in

Bruce, $150,000 to the Nipissing road, $100,000 to the Northern, and $350,000 to the Credit Valley. Hamilton backed the Hamilton and North-Western by $200,000, London gave the London, Huron and Bruce $150,000, and generous Kingston gave to the Kingston and Pembroke over $300,000. Counties like Elgin and Simcoe, Grey, and Frontenac offered from $150,000 to $300,000, while from townships alone the Wellington, Grey and Bruce received $680,000. Montreal and Quebec each helped the North Shore by a gift of a million dollars; Ottawa county's $200,000 and the parish of Canrobert's $1000 were equally sought; while to a lesser degree the Maritime Provinces showed the same tendency.

the United States.   In 1867 the Grand Trunk
and the Great Western agreed to maintain
rates, pool certain traffic receipts, refrain
from competitive building, and co-operate in
service. The agreement broke down; another
was made in 1876, only to fail in turn. More
effective measures had to be adopted.

The outstanding achievement of the period,
however, was the building of the Intercolonial.
It had been projected largely in order to make
closer union between the provinces possible,
but, as it turned out, it was Confederation
that brought the Intercolonial, not the Intercolonial that brought Confederation.

After the breakdown of the negotiations in
London in 1852, each province had turned to
its own tasks. But each in building its own
roads had provided possible links in the
future Intercolonial chain. In Canada the
Grand Trunk ran to a point 120 miles east of
Quebec ; in New Brunswick, St John was
connected with both the east and west boun-
daries of the province ; in Nova Scotia, a road
ran north from Halifax as far as Truro. A
gap of nearly five hundred miles between
Rivière du Loup and Truro remained. To
bridge this wilderness seemed beyond the

private or public resources of the divided provinces. Unanimous on one point only, they once more turned to the British government. In 1857 and 1858 dispatches and deputations sought aid, but sought it in vain. When the Civil War broke out in the United States, official British sympathy was given to the South, and the *Trent* affair showed how near Britain and the North were to war, a war which would at once have exposed the isolated colonies to American attack. The military argument for closer connection then took on new weight with the British government, and it proposed, to a joint delegation in 1861, to revert to its offer of ten years earlier—to guarantee a colonial loan for a railway by an approved route. The colonies opposed the demand for a sinking fund, and again agreement was postponed. In 1863 Canada suggested that, as the British government had made an approved route an essential condition, a definite survey and selection should be undertaken forthwith. It was agreed that a commission of three engineers should be selected, one nominated by Canada, one by New Brunswick and Nova Scotia, and one by Great Britain. Canada nominated Sandford Fleming, a distinguished Scottish-Canadian engineer, who had been connected with the Northern and other Upper Canada enterprises. The other authorities paid him the compliment of naming him as their representative also, to facilitate the work. During the progress of the survey negotiations for the union of the provinces had begun, and when Confederation came about in 1867, the building of the Intercolonial at the common expense of the Dominion, with an imperial guarantee to the extent of £3,000,000, was one of the conditions of union. The old difficulty as to the route through New Brunswick was still to be settled. Again western and southern New Brunswick struggled against the north and against far east Quebec; again Halifax and St John found plausible arguments to uphold their respective interests. Finally, the views of Sir George Cartier and Peter Mitchell triumphed in the Cabinet councils, and in March 1868 the engineer-in-chief advised the selection of the roundabout Bay of Chaleurs route—roughly 'Major Robinson's line'—ostensibly because safer from American attack, nearer possible steamship connection with Europe, and no worse, if no better, than the other routes in potentialities of local traffic.

The construction was entrusted in December

1868 to a commission of four ; six years later the minister of Public Works took over direct control. Sandford Fleming remained engineer-in-chief for the building as well as for the survey. Tenders were submitted for the construction of the whole road, but the government decided to award the contract in small sections. The road was not completed as speedily as had been expected. Difficulties arose, expected and unexpected—cuttings in heavy rock, sliding clay banks, extensive swamps, lack of rock bottom for heavy bridges. Contractor after contractor found that he had underestimated the task, and went bankrupt or threw up the contract. Sometimes the contract was relet, sometimes the government completed it by day work. At last, on July 1, 1876, nine years after Confederation, the five hundred miles between Truro and Rivière du Loup were opened for traffic throughout. In the meantime the Dominion had taken over the Nova Scotia, New Brunswick, and Prince Edward Island government roads. In 1876 there were in all 950 miles of railway under the control of the Dominion government, as against 4268 miles of private lines.

CHAPTER VII

THE CANADIAN PACIFIC—BEGINNINGS

On March 3, 1841, Sir George Simpson, governor-in-chief of the Hudson's Bay Company's domains, left London on a journey round the world. All the resources of a powerful and well-organized corporation were at his disposal, and his own reputation for rapid travelling gave assurance that on the actual journey not an hour would be lost. A fortnight's sail brought him from Liverpool to Halifax, and thence he journeyed by steamer to Boston, by rail to Nashua, by coach to Concord, and by sleigh to Montreal. The portage railway from St John to Laprairie was on his route, but it was not open in winter.

From Montreal Sir George and his party set out on May 4 in two light thirty-foot canoes, each carrying a crew of twelve or fourteen men. At top speed they worked their way up the Ottawa and the Mattawa out to Lake Nipissing, and down the French River into Georgian Bay. They camped every night at sunset, and rose each morning at one. Their tireless Canadian and Iroquois voyageurs worked eighteen hours a day, paddling swiftly through smooth water, wading through shallows, or towing the canoes through the lesser rapids, or portaging once to a dozen times a day round the more difficult ones. Each voyageur was ready to shoulder his 180 pounds, strapped to his forehead, or to ferry passengers ashore on his back. They reached Sault Ste Marie on May 16, only to find Lake Superior still frozen. They picked their way very slowly through the opening rifts along the shore, made the Company's post at Fort William in eleven days, exchanged their large canoes for smaller craft, and paddled and portaged through the endless network of river and lake to Fort Garry, which they reached on June 10, thirty-eight days out from Montreal.

From Fort Garry a fresh start was made on July 3, on horseback, with baggage sent ahead in lumbering Red River carts. Past Fort Ellice and Fort Carlton, they pushed on with fresh supplies of horses at the topmost speed that the limitations of their convoy of carts would permit. Band after band of Plains

SIR GEORGE SIMPSON

From a print in the John Ross Robertson Collection,
Toronto Public Library

Indians, adorned with war-paint and scalp-locks, crossed their trail, but mosquito and sand-fly proved more troublesome. The travellers passed a band of emigrants making slowly for the Columbia, and everywhere found countless herds of buffalo. In three weeks from Fort Garry they reached Fort Edmonton. Here forty-five fresh horses were in readiness for riding, pack-horses took the place of carts, and the journey was continued to the south-west. The Rockies were crossed through Kootenay Pass, and at last—after many a halt to find straying horses, and after continuous annoyance from mosquitoes and venomous insects 'which in size and appearance might have been mistaken for a cross between the bulldog and the house-fly '—Fort Colville on the Columbia was reached on August 18. Their long horseback ride was over. Favoured by wonderfully fine weather, in the saddle eleven to twelve hours a day, they had made their way through open prairie and rolling plain, tangled thicket and burning forest and rushing river, and had covered the two thousand miles from Fort Garry in six weeks and five days. From Fort Colville they reached the waters of the Pacific at Fort Vancouver (Washington) in another six days. The continent had been crossed in twelve weeks of actual travelling.

Sir George Simpson's journey stood as the record for many a year. For a generation after his day the scattered travellers from Red River westward were compelled to rely on saddle-horse and plains cart and canoe. From Montreal and Toronto the railway could be utilized as far as Collingwood, and thence the steamer to Port Arthur. Then for a time the government opened up a summer route to the Red River, beginning it in 1869 and maintaining it until 1876. The Dawson route, as it was called, included forty-five miles of wagon-road from Port Arthur to Lake Shebandowan, then over three hundred miles of water travel, with a dozen portages, and again ninety-five miles of wagon-road from the Lake of the Woods to Fort Garry.[1] In 1870 it took ninety-five days to transport troops from Toronto to Fort Garry over this route. Such make-shifts could not serve for long. South of the

[1] 'Lord Strathcona may still remember the man who came into his office at Winnipeg and said : " Look at me ; ain't I a healthy sight? I 've come by the government water route from Thunder Bay, and it 's taken me twenty-five days to do it. During that time I 've been half-starved on victuals I wouldn't give a swampy Indian. The water used to pour into my bunk at nights, and the boat was so leaky that every bit of baggage I 've got is

border the railway was rapidly pushing westward, and in the new nation of the north, as
well, its time had come.

Ever after the coming of the locomotive, it
needed only imagination and a map to see all
British North America clamped by an iron
band. Engineers like Bonnycastle and Synge
and Carmichael-Smyth wrote of the possibility in the forties. Politicians found in the
theme matter for admirable after-dinner per-
orations—colonial governors like Harvey in
1847, colonial secretaries like Lytton and
Carnarvon in the fifties, and colonial premiers
like Joseph Howe, who declared in Halifax in
1851: 'I believe that many in this room will
live to hear the whistle of the steam-engine
in the passes of the Rocky Mountains, and to
make the journey from Halifax to the Pacific
in five or six days.' Promoters were not lacking. In 1851 Allan Macdonnell of Toronto
sought a charter and a subsidy for a road to
the Pacific, and the Canadian authorities, in

water-logged and ruined. I've broke my arm and sprained my
ankle helping to carry half a dozen trunks over a dozen portages,
and when I refused to take a paddle on one of the boats, an
Ottawa Irishman told me to go to hell, and said that if I gave
him any more of my damned chat he'd let me get off and walk
to Winnipeg.'"—W. L. Grant in *Geographical Journal*, October
1911, p. 365.

declining, expressed their opinion that the
scheme was not visionary and their hope that
some day Great Britain and the United States
might undertake it jointly.   Seven years later
the same promoter secured a charter for the
Northwest Transportation, Navigation, and
Railway Company, to operate between Lake
Superior and the Fraser river, but could get
no backing; four years previously John Young,
A. N. Morin, A. T. Galt, and John A. Poor
had petitioned in vain for a similar charter.
Then in 1862, on behalf of the Red River
Settlement, Sandford Fleming prepared an
elaborate memorial on the subject.   Edwin
Watkin, of the Grand Trunk, negotiated with
the Hudson's Bay Company for right of way
and other facilities, but the project proved too
vast for his resources.

Two things were needed before dreams on
paper could become facts in steel—national
unity and international rivalry.   Years before
Confederation, such far-seeing Canadians as
William M'Dougall and George Brown had
pressed for the annexation of the British
territories beyond the Lakes.   After Confederation, all speed was made to buy out the
sovereign rights of the Hudson's Bay Company.   Then came the first Riel Rebellion, to

SIR SANDFORD FLEMING

From a photograph by Topley

bring home the need of a western road, as the *Trent* affair had brought home the need of the Intercolonial. The decisive political factor came into play in 1870, when British Columbia entered the federation. Its less than ten thousand white inhabitants—deeming themselves citizens of no mean country, and kept to their demands by the urging of an indefatigable Englishman, Alfred Waddington—made the construction of an overland railway an indispensable condition of union, and Sir John Macdonald courageously accepted their terms.

The other factor, international rivalry, exercised its influence about the same time. In the United States the railway had rapidly pushed westward, but had halted before the deserts and the mountains lying between the Mississippi and the Pacific. The rivalry of pro-slavery and anti-slavery parties in Congress long brought to deadlock all plans of public aid to either southern or northern route. Then the Civil War broke the deadlock : the need of binding the West to the side of the North created a strong public demand for a Pacific road, and Congress, so stimulated, and further lubricated by the payment, as is proven, of at least $476,000 in bribes, gave lavish loans and grants of land. The Central Pacific, working from Sacramento, and the Union Pacific, starting from Omaha, met near Ogden in Utah in 1869—or rather here the rails met, for the rival companies, eager to earn the high subsidy given for mountain construction, had actually graded two hundred superfluous miles in parallel lines. In 1871 the Southern Pacific and the Texas Pacific were fighting for subsidies, and Jay Cooke was promoting the Northern Pacific. The young Dominion was stirred by ambition to emulate its powerful neighbour.

These factors, then, brought the question of a railway to the Pacific on Canadian soil within the range of practical politics. Important questions remained to be settled. During the parliamentary session of 1871 the government of Sir John Macdonald decided that the road should be built by a company, not by the state, that it should be aided by liberal subsidies in cash and in land, and, to meet British Columbia's insistent terms, that it should be begun within two, and completed within ten, years. The Opposition protested that this latter provision was uncalled for and would bankrupt the Dominion, but the government carried its point, though it was forced to hedge later by a stipulation—not included in the formal resolutions—that the annual expenditure should be such as not to press unduly upon the Dominion's resources.

The first task was to survey the vast wilderness between the Ottawa valley and the Pacific, and to find, if possible, a feasible route. So able an explorer and engineer as Captain Palliser, appointed by the British government to report upon the country west of the Lakes, had declared in 1863, after four years of careful labour in the field, that, thanks to the choice of the 49th parallel as Canada's boundary, there was no possibility of ever building a transcontinental railway exclusively through British territory. The man chosen for the task of achieving this impossibility was Sandford Fleming. Appointed engineer-in-chief in 1871, he was for nine years in charge of the surveys, though for half that time his duties on the Intercolonial absorbed much of his energy. Mr Fleming possessed an unusual gift of literary style, and his reports upon the work of his staff gave the people of Canada a very clear idea of the difficulties to be encountered. His friend, the Rev. George M. Grant, who accompanied him in a rapid reconnaissance in 1872, gave, in his book

Ocean to Ocean, a vivid and heartening record of the realities and the promise that he
saw.

It had been decided, in order to hold the
balance even between Montreal and Toronto,
to make the proposed Pacific road begin at
some angle of Lake Nipissing. From that
point nearly to the Red River there stretched
a thousand miles of woodland, rugged and
rock-strewn, covered by a network of countless
lakes and rivers, interspersed with seemingly
bottomless swamps or muskegs—a wilderness
which no white man had ever passed through
from end to end. Then came the level prairie
and a great rolling plain rising to the south-
west in three successive steppes, and cut by
deep watercourses. But it was the third or
mountain section which presented the most
serious engineering difficulties. Four hundred miles from the Pacific coast, and roughly
parallel, ran the towering Rocky Mountains,
some of whose peaks rose fifteen thousand feet.
Beyond stretched a vast plateau, three or
four thousand feet above sea-level, intersected
by rivers which had cut deep chasms or, to the
northward, wide sheltered valleys. Between
this plateau and the coast the Cascades interposed, rivalling the Rockies in height and

rising sheer from the ocean, which thrust in deep fiord channels. At the head of some one of these fiords must be found the western terminus.

Early in the survey a practicable route was found throughout. Striking across the wilderness from Lake Nipissing to Lake Superior at the river Pic, the line might skirt the shore of the lake to Fort William, or it might run northerly through what is now known as the clay belt, with Fort William and the lake made accessible by a branch. Continuing westward to the Red River at Selkirk, with Winnipeg on a branch line to the south, the projected line crossed Lake Manitoba at the Narrows, and then struck out northwesterly, through what was then termed the 'Fertile Belt,' till the Yellowhead Pass was reached. Here the Rockies could be easily pierced; but once through the engineer was faced by the huge flanking range of the Cariboo Mountains, in which repeated explorations failed to find a gap. But at the foot of the towering barrier lay a remarkable deep-set valley four hundred miles in length, in which northwestward ran the Fraser and southeastward the Canoe and the Columbia. By following the Fraser to its great southward bend, and then striking west, a terminus on Bute or Dean Inlet might be reached, while the valley of the Canoe and the Albreda would give access to the North Thompson as far as Kamloops, whence the road might run down the Thompson and the lower Fraser to Burrard Inlet. The latter route, on the whole, was preferred.

While this route was feasible, the mountain portion promised to be extremely expensive. This factor, together with the uncertainty of government policy and the desire of Victoria to have the road built to Bute Inlet and thence, by a bridge across Valdes Strait, carried down to Esquimalt, made it necessary to seek untiringly, year after year, for alternative routes. The only important change made, however, until after 1880, was the deflection of the line south of Lake Manitoba to serve existing settlements.

Who was to build the road ? It would be a tremendous task for either the government or the private capitalists of a nation of four million people. The United States had not begun its Pacific roads till it had over thirty millions of people, and wealth and experience to correspond. It was estimated that the Canadian road would cost $100,000,000, and it was certain that the engineering difficulties

would be staggering. In Canada few roads
had paid the shareholders, and though some
had profited the contractors, the new enterprise meant such a plunge in the dark that
contractors and promoters alike hesitated.
In the United States, however, the Pacific
roads had proved gold-mines for their promoters. The land-grants were valuable, and
the privilege of granting contracts to dummy
construction companies controlled by themselves and thus reaping larger profits was still
greater.

It was not to be wondered at, therefore,
that the first offer came from American capitalists. Alfred Waddington, enthusiast rather
than practical promoter, sought at Ottawa a
charter for the road he had done so much to
secure, but his bill went no further than a
first reading. At Ottawa he was met by
G. W. M'Mullen, a Canadian residing in
Chicago, who was visiting the Dominion on a
canal deputation. M'Mullen became interested, and with his Chicago partners endeavoured to enlist the aid of the men behind the
Northern Pacific—Jay Cooke, General Cass,
W. B. Ogden, T. A. Scott, and others.[1]

[1] The Northern Pacific was at many stages in its history
closely connected with Canadian affairs. It had originally been

M'Mullen soon found that Waddington had exaggerated his influence, and that the government was not yet prepared to discuss terms. Sir Francis Hincks, stormy petrel of railway building, whom Sir John Macdonald had just made his finance minister, suggested to Sir Hugh Allan of Montreal that he should get into touch with these Americans and provide the substantial Canadian interest which was essential.

Sir Hugh Allan was then the foremost business man in Canada. He was head of the great Allan steamship line, and had become interested in railways shortly before, when rumours of the intention of the Grand Trunk to establish a rival steamship line to Great

projected in New England: the first proposal was to use the Central Vermont and a Canadian road to be built or acquired as the eastern links, then, crossing into Michigan, the railway was to strike northwestward to the Pacific. When control fell into the hands of New York and Philadelphia interests, these plans were dropped, but later the new management negotiated with Governor Archibald of Manitoba, as well as with Sir John Macdonald, to endeavour to put through an international road, the first section running through Canada to Sault Ste Marie, the second through Michigan and Minnesota, the third through the Canadian plains, and the fourth through the Rockies to the sea on American territory. Nothing came of the negotiations, though it may be noted that the Canadian Pacific to-day has carried out precisely this plan, in addition to its all-Canadian line:

Britain had led him to assist in promoting the North Shore from Quebec westward, to compete with the Grand Trunk and ensure traffic for his steamers. He now opened negotiations with the American capitalists through M'Mullen, came to terms, and then sought associates in Canada. Here difficulties arose: Ontario objected that Allan's control would mean a Quebec rather than an Ontario terminus, and that the Northern Pacific directors with whom he was associated were simply conspiring to get control of the Canadian road, in order to delay its construction and prevent it becoming a rival to their own northerly route. Sir George Cartier, too, powerful in the Cabinet and salaried solicitor of the Grand Trunk, was a stumbling-block; he declared himself emphatically opposed to control by any ' *sacrée compagnie américaine.*' But Sir Hugh, believing much in money and little in men, resolved to buy his way through. He soon started a backfire in Quebec which brought Cartier to terms. Ontario rivalry was harder to control: D. L. Macpherson and other Toronto men organized the Interoceanic Railway Company to oppose Allan's Canada Pacific Company. Both companies sought charters and aid. Allan pretended to drop his American associates; Macpherson charged that the connection still existed. The government endeavoured to bring about an amalgamation, with Allan as president, and, failing this, to organize a new company. In the meantime Allan was spending money so freely that even his New York associates were astounded. The Dominion elections were held in August 1872, and Macdonald, Cartier, and Langevin drew heavily on Allan's funds, $162,500 in all, with a promise from Cartier that 'any amount which you or your Company shall advance for that purpose shall be re-couped to you.' After the election a new company, the Canadian Pacific, was organized, with representative men from each province as directors; and the new board, of its own motion, it was declared, elected Allan president. To this company the government granted a charter, promised a subsidy of thirty million dollars and fifty million acres of land, but insisted upon excluding the American interests. Allan acquiesced, and, repaying the advances made, informed New York that negotiations were ended. M'Mullen and his associates, angry at this treatment, conveyed rumours to Opposition leaders, and finally Allan's confidential correspondence, stolen by a clerk in the office of J. J. C. Abbott, Allan's solicitor, was made public.[1] The fat was in the fire.

With the political controversy which followed we are not here concerned. In Sir John Macdonald's defence it could be said, that though Allan's money was taken no

[1] This correspondence will be found in the Journals of the House of Commons, vol. vii, 1873. In no other documents available to the public has the connection between politics and railway promoting in Canada been made so evident. The following are a few brief extracts from letters addressed by Sir Hugh Allan to various American associates during 1872:

Thinking that as I had taken up the project there must be something very good in it, a very formidable opposition was organized in Toronto, which for want of a better took as their cry 'No foreign influence; no Yankee dictation; no Northern Pacific to choke off our Canadian Pacific,' and others equally sensible. . . . I was forced to drop ostensibly from our organization every American name, and put in reliable people on this side in place of them. . . . Mr M'Mullen was desirous of securing the inferior members of the Government, and entered into engagements of which I did not approve, as I thought it was only a waste of powder and shot. On a calm view of the situation I satisfied myself that the decision of the question must ultimately be in the hands of one man, and that man was Sir George E. Cartier, the leader of the French party, which held the balance of power between the other factions. . . . It was evident that some means must be adopted to bring the influence of this compact body of men to bear in our favour, and as soon as I made up my mind what to do, I did not lose a moment in following it up. A railroad from Montreal to Ottawa, through the French country, north of the Ottawa river, has

special favours were shown in the contract made ; and that all that Allan secured by the government's victory was the certainty that the railway project would not be postponed or dropped altogether, and that he would be given control. Sir Hugh Allan had said with much force : ' The plans I propose are in themselves the best for the interests of the Dominion, and in urging them on the public I am really doing a most patriotic action.' Undoubtedly Sir John Macdonald sincerely held a similar opinion.

long been desired by the French inhabitants ; but Cartier, who is a salaried solicitor of the Grand Trunk road, to which this would be an opposition, has interposed difficulties, and by his influence prevented it being built. . . . The plans I propose are in themselves the best for the interests of the Dominion, and in urging them on the public I am really doing a most patriotic action. But even in that view, means must be used to influence the public, and I employed several young French lawyers to write it up in their own news-papers. I subscribed a controlling influence in the stock, and proceeded to subsidize the newspapers themselves, both editors and proprietors. I went to the country through which the road would pass, and called on many of the in-habitants. I visited the priests and made friends of them, and I employed agents to go among the principal people and talk it up. I then began to hold public meetings, and attended to them myself, making frequent speeches in French to them, showing them where their true interests lay . . . and I formed a committee to influence the members of the Legis-lature. This succeeded so well that in a short time it had 27 out of 45 on whom I could rely, and the electors of the

The Allan Company gave up its charter, unable to raise capital in face of financial depression and political upheaval. The Liberal party, led by Alexander Mackenzie, and swept into power by a wave of popular indignation, first endeavoured to induce other capitalists to take up the work. But the government's offers of $10,000 in cash and of 20,000 acres of land for each mile, plus an undetermined guarantee, had no takers in the years of depression that followed. Mackenzie then decided that the government should

ward in this city, which Cartier himself represents, notified him that unless the contract for the Pacific Railway was given in the interests of Lower Canada he need not present himself for re-election. . . .

The policy adopted has been quite successful, the strong French influence I succeeded in obtaining has proved sufficient to control the elections, and as soon as the Government realized this fact, which they were unwilling to admit and slow to see, they opened negotiations with me. . . . Yesterday we entered into an agreement, by which the Government bound itself to form a Company of Canadians, only according to my wishes. That this Company will make me President, and that I and my friends will get a majority of the stock, and that the contract for building the railroad will be given to this Company, in terms of the Act of Parliament. Americans are to be carefully excluded in the fear that they will sell it to the Union [sic] Pacific, but I fancy we can get over that some way or other. This position has not been attained without large payments of money. I have already paid over $200,000, and will have at least $100,000 more to pay.

itself build the road.   He planned to build at first only the indispensable sections, using the waterways wherever possible, and hoped, but in vain, to secure British Columbia's consent to an extension of the time set for completion. His first step was to subsidize the Canada Central, which ran from Ottawa via Carleton Place to Pembroke, to extend its line as far as Lake Nipissing, in order to connect with the proposed eastern terminus of the Pacific road, and to award a contract (it was afterwards cancelled) for a branch from this junction point to Georgian Bay.   Passing by for the time the country north of Lake Superior, he next let contracts for the greater part of the distance between Fort William and Selkirk and for a road from Selkirk to Emerson, on the Manitoba border.   Here connection was to be made with an American line, the St Paul and Pacific, of which more will be heard presently.

When Mackenzie left office in 1878 the work of location or construction was well advanced in all three sections.   For two years the new administration of Sir John Macdonald carried on the same policy of government construction at a moderate pace.   The work in hand was continued and the gaps in the road between Port Arthur and Selkirk were put under contract. The line was made to pass through Winnipeg—instead of striking west from Selkirk, as the engineers had previously advised, and thus side-tracking the ambitious city growing up around old Fort Garry. Contracts were let for two hundred miles of the extension westward from Winnipeg. Two seasons passed before the new government could make up its mind as to the British Columbia section. Late in 1879 it decided to adhere to the route chosen under the Mackenzie administration, through the Yellowhead Pass, down the Thompson and the Fraser to Port Moody on Burrard Inlet. The difficult section from Yale, the head of navigation on the Fraser, to Savona's Ferry, near Kamloops, was shortly afterwards placed under contract.

The ten years' time allotted for the construction of the Canadian Pacific was nearly gone and there was little completed work to show. Hard times, depression in the railway world, changes of government and political upheavals, disputes as to route and terminus, had delayed construction. The building of the link north of Lake Superior, necessary for all-rail connection between East and West on Canadian territory, had been indefinitely postponed.

Something had been done, it is true. Manitoba was being linked up with the East by a road south to Minnesota and by another line to the head of Lake Superior, and a start had been made in British Columbia. Some day, under some administration, the gaps would be filled up and the promise to British Columbia would be redeemed.

Suddenly, in June 1880, Sir John Macdonald, speaking at Bath, made the announcement that a group of capitalists had offered to build the road, on terms which would ensure that in the end it would not cost Canada a single farthing. Four months later a contract was signed in Ottawa by which the Canadian Pacific Syndicate undertook to build and operate the whole road. An entirely new turn had been given to the situation, and the most important chapter in Canada's railway annals, if not in her national life, had been begun.

CHAPTER VIII

BUILDING THE CANADIAN PACIFIC

In the months and years that followed, no men were so much in the mind and speech of the Canadian public as the members of the new syndicate. The leading members were a remarkable group of men. Probably never in the history of railway building, not even in the case of the ' Big Four ' who built the Central Pacific—Huntingdon, Stanford, Crocker, and Hopkins—had the call of the railway brought together in a single enterprise men of such outstanding individuality, of such ability and persistence, and destined for success so notable.

The Canadian Pacific was not their first joint enterprise. It was the direct outcome of a daring venture in connection with a bankrupt Minnesota railway, which had brought them wealth beyond their wildest dreams, and had definitely turned their thoughts to railway work.

Early in the settlement of the northwestern

states the need of railways, and of state aid to railways, was widely realized.   In 1857 Congress gave the territory of Minnesota a large grant of public lands to use in bonusing railway building, and in the same year the legislature of the territory incorporated a company, the Minnesota and Pacific, to build from Stillwater through St Paul and St Anthony's Falls (Minneapolis) to Red River points.   The state gave the new company millions of acres of land and a cash subsidy, municipalities offered bonuses, and a small amount of stock was subscribed locally.   Five years passed, and not a mile had been completed.   The company, looted into insolvency by fraudulent construction company contracts, was reorganized as the St Paul and Pacific, heir to the old company's assets but not to its liabilities, and a beginning was made once more.   Trusting Dutch bondholders lent over twenty millions, and by 1871 the road reached Breckenridge on the Red River, two hundred and seventeen miles from St Paul.   Again a halt came. Russell Sage and his associates in control had once more looted the treasury.   The Dutch bondholders, through their agent, John S. Kennedy, a New York banker, applied for a receiver, and in 1873 one Jesse P. Farley was appointed by the court. It seemed that the angry settlers might whistle in vain for their road.

In St Paul at that time there lived two Canadians who saw the opportunity. The elder, Norman W. Kittson, had been Hudson Bay agent and head of a transportation company on the Red River. The younger, James J. Hill, an Ontario farm-boy who had gone west while still in his teens, owned a coal and wood yard in St Paul, and had a share in the transportation company. Neither had the capital or the financial connection required to take hold of the bankrupt company, but they kept on thinking of it day and night. Soon a third man joined their ranks, Donald A. Smith. A Highland lad who had come to Canada at eighteen, Donald Smith had spent a generation in the service of the Hudson's Bay Company, mainly in the dreary wilds of Labrador and on the shores of Hudson Bay. When in 1871 he became chief commissioner of the organization he had served so long and so well, it seemed to most men that he was definitely settled in his life work and probably near the height of his career. But Fate knew, and Donald Smith knew, that his career was only beginning. Coming down from the north each year by the Red River to St Paul, on his way east, he talked over the railway situation with Hill and Kittson. The more they talked the greater grew their faith in the country and the railroad. It was a faith, however, that few in the moneyed East shared with them. It had been the smashing of the rival road, the Northern Pacific, in 1873, that had given the signal for the brief panic and the long depression of the seventies. The Minnesota road itself had twice become bankrupt. The legislature would undoubtedly soon declare the land-grant forfeited, unless the construction promised was completed. To fill the cup, in the middle seventies Minnesota and the neighbouring lands were visited by unprecedented swarms of grasshoppers or Rocky Mountain locusts. Swarming down from the plateau lands of the Rockies in columns miles high, covering the ground from horizon to horizon, they swept resistlessly forward, devouring every green thing in their way. When they had passed, hundreds of deserted shacks stood silent witnesses to the settlers' despair.

It was in 1876 that the further allies needed came from the East. Thirty years earlier George Stephen, a younger cousin of Donald Smith, had left his Highland hills to seek his

LORD STRATHCONA

From a photograph by Lafayette, London

fortune in London, and after a short apprenticeship there had gone still farther afield, joining an uncle in Montreal. He rose rapidly to a foremost place in the wholesale trade of Montreal ; selling led him into manufacturing, and manufacturing into financial activities. In 1876 he became president of the Bank of Montreal. Associated with him in the same bank was still another shrewd, forth-faring Scot, Richard B. Angus, who had risen steadily in its service until appointed to succeed E. H. King as general manager in 1869.

A lawsuit in connection with the bank's affairs took both Stephen and Angus to Chicago in 1876. A week's adjournment left them with unwonted leisure. A toss of a coin sent them to St Paul rather than to St Louis to spend the week. Smith had already spoken of the project while in Montreal, but at that distance caution had prevailed. Now Stephen, who had never before seen the prairie, was immensely taken with the rich, deep soil he saw before him. He knew from reading and experience that grasshopper plagues did not last for ever. He decided, therefore, to join in the attempt to get control of the Minnesota road and its land-grant, and the famous group was complete.

Once George Stephen had made up his mind, little time was ever lost.   He sailed for Europe and interviewed the Amsterdam committee in charge of the Dutch bondholders' interests, Messrs Chouet, Weetjin and Kirkhoven. They despaired of ever seeing their money back, and were weary of being assessed by the receiver for funds to keep the road together. Stephen left Amsterdam with an option in his pocket, given for the sum of one guilder, agreeing to sell him the Dutch bonds for something like the amount of the unpaid interest, and agreeing, further, to wait until six months after reorganization for part of the payment.   The next step was to provide the cash required for immediate necessities.   About $300,000 was put up by the members of the group.[1] Money was borrowed from the Bank of Montreal, $280,000 in the first advance, and something under $700,000 in all, as Stephen stated to inquiring shareholders at the bank's annual meeting in 1880.   Money was advanced to the receiver to complete the most necessary extensions, those required to save the land-grant and that necessary to reach the Canadian

[1] Stephen, Smith, Hill, and Kennedy each took one share, and Kittson half a share ; and later Angus, after leaving the service of the bank to go with the railway, took the remaining half-share.

border to join the government road being built
south from Winnipeg. The threatened for-
feiture of the land-grant was thus averted for
a time. Then the bonds were purchased for
$6,780,000, the floating obligations and part
of the stock were bought up, and the mortgage which secured the bonds was foreclosed.
The assets were bought by the new company
organized for the purpose, the St Paul, Minneapolis and Manitoba, of which George Stephen
was president, R. B. Angus vice-president, and
James J. Hill general manager. Thus in June
1879 the whole system, comprising six hundred
and sixty-seven miles of railway, of which five
hundred and sixty-five were completed, and
the land-grant of two and a half million acres,
came into the possession of the little group.[1]

The after fortunes of the road, which ten
years later expanded into the Great Northern
of to-day, do not concern us here. It is only
necessary to recount that the harvest reaped

[1] Not all were willing to attribute to courage and luck alone
the full success of this stroke. Some Dutch bondholders, inde-
pendently of the committee, asserted that Kennedy had not played
fair, and Farley, the receiver of the road, sued Hill for a share of
the profits which he alleged had been promised for his collusion.
In repeated trials Farley was unable to produce evidence satisfactory to the courts, which held that in any case his claim must
be rejected because 'based on inherent turpitude.'

by the adventurers [1] put the tales of El Dorado to shame. A few days after control of the railway had been assured, the grasshoppers had risen in flight, and Minnesota knew them no more. Settlers swarmed in, the railroad platforms were jammed with land-seekers, and between the land-buyers of to-day and the wheat-shippers of to-morrow the owners of the once discredited railway saw their coffers fill to overflowing. In 1879 they divided among themselves the whole fifteen millions of stock issued, floating sixteen millions of bonds for extension and equipment. For three years they took no dividends, letting the profits go to further building. Then in 1882 another $2,000,000 stock was issued, and in 1883 a deferred dividend came in the shape of a $9,000,000 issue of bonds, or, rather, the stock-holders sold to themselves a $10,000,000 issue for ten cents on the dollar. Aside entirely from interest and dividends, the stockholders of the Great Northern in the seventeen years following 1889 were presented with over $300,000,000 of interest - bearing securities.

---

[1] 'Most men who have really lived have had, in some shape, their great adventure. This railway is mine' (James J. Hill, in Valedictory to the Shareholders of the Great Northern, July 1, 1912).

All the railway annals of the United States cannot present a duplicate of the startling success attained by these four or five Canadians and their associates.[1]

These were the men to whom the Canadian government turned when the minister of Railways, Sir Charles Tupper, urged them to unload upon a private company the burden of completing the road to the Pacific. 'Catch them before they invest their profits,' was the advice of Sir John's most intimate adviser, that shrewd Eastern Townships politician, John Henry Pope. Probably they came halfway. They knew the West as well as any men, and with their road built to the Canadian boundary and with a traffic arrangement beyond to Winnipeg, they were already in the field. Of all the group Stephen was most reluctant to undertake the new enterprise, but he was assured by his associates that the burdens of management would be shared by all. The government had also approached Duncan M'Intyre, a Montreal capitalist who controlled the Canada Central, running from Brockville by way of Ottawa to Pembroke,

---

[1] It was from their St Paul investment that the leading men in the group secured the basis and the bulk of their great fortunes; the Canadian Pacific added little to their coffers.

and under construction from that point to Callender, the eastern end of the Canadian Pacific main line. He was more than willing to link up this railway with the larger project, and the group was formed.

They debated the question with the government early in 1880. It was felt, however, that negotiations could not be concluded in Canada. More capital would be needed than even these new-fledged millionaires could or would furnish, and nowhere was capital so abundant as in London. In July, therefore, Sir John Macdonald, Sir Charles Tupper, and John Henry Pope sailed for London, accompanied by George Stephen and Duncan M'Intyre. London capitalists did not bite as freely as anticipated. Barings and Rothschilds alike were chary about the enterprise. Sir Henry Tyler, president of the Grand Trunk, was approached, and agreed to build if the link north of Lake Superior were omitted in favour of a line through the United States, south of the lake, a condition which Sir John, strongly urged on by Tupper, would not accept. An arrangement might have been made with a London group, but only on condition of a four per cent guarantee for twelve years, another condition which, less wisely, was also rejected. In the

LORD MOUNT STEPHEN

From a photograph by Wood and Henry, Dufftown
By courtesy of Sir William Van Horne

end the quest proved unavailing. It is true
that the Paris firm of Cohen, Reinach and
Co. entered the syndicate, and that the
London house of Morton, Rose and Co.
also joined. It was really, however, the New
York end of that firm, Morton, Bliss and
Co., which was interested. Contrary to the
general impression, the fact is, that though
most of the shares when issued eventually
drifted into English hands, no English financiers shared in the building of the Canadian
Pacific until it was within one hundred days
of completion. Perhaps, in view of the Grand
Trunk's record, it was as well that the men on
this side of the Atlantic were to be thrown on
their own resources from the start, and given the
chance for bigness which responsibility brings.

Back to Ottawa the pilgrims came, and
there on October 21, 1880, the contract was
signed by Charles Tupper for the government
and by George Stephen, Duncan M'Intyre,
James J. Hill, John S. Kennedy, Morton, Rose
and Co. of London, and Cohen, Reinach and
Co. of Paris. Donald A. Smith's name was
not there. It was only two years since he and
Sir John, on the floor of the House of Commons,
had called each other ' liar ' and ' coward '
and any other sufficiently strong epithet they

could put their tongues to, and it was to be a few years more before the two Highlanders could cover their private feud with a coating of elaborate cordiality. So, to preserve appearances, Smith's interest was kept a secret—but a very open one.

When parliament met in December 1880 the contract was laid before it. The terms were princely. For constructing some nineteen hundred miles the syndicate were to be given free and complete the seven hundred and ten miles under construction by the government,[1] $25,000,000 in cash, and 25,000,000 acres of selected land in the Fertile Belt. They were promised exemptions from import duties on construction materials, from taxes on land for twenty years after the patents were issued and on stock and other property for ever, and exemption from regulation of rates until ten per cent per annum was earned on the capital. Assurance was given that for twenty years no competitive roads connecting with the western states would be chartered : ' no line of railway south of the Canadian Pacific, except such line as shall run southwest or to the westward of southwest, nor to be within fifteen miles

[1] Including the Yale-Port Moody section, not yet formally under contract.

of latitude 49°.' Ten years were given to complete the task, and a million dollars were deposited as security.

The contract was received by Blake, then leader of the Opposition, and his followers with a unanimous shout of disapproval. During the Christmas recess Blake endeavoured to raise the country against it. A rival syndicate was hastily organized, with Sir William Howland, A. R. M'Master, William Hendrie, A. T. Wood, Allan Gilmour, George A. Cox, P. Larkin, James M'Laren, Alexander Gibson, and other well-known capitalists at its head. After depositing $1,400,000 in chartered banks as evidence of good faith, they offered to build the road for $3,000,000 and 3,000,000 acres less, to pay duty on all supplies imported, and to abandon the monopoly clause, the exemptions from taxation, and the exemption from rate regulation. With this weapon to brandish Blake gave the government proposal no respite, but on a straight party vote the contract was ratified by parliament and received the formal royal assent in February 1881.

It was in many ways unfortunate that from the outset the Canadian Pacific project was made the football of party politics, but it was perhaps inevitable. The first duty of an Opposition is to oppose, and even if some good measures are factitiously resisted, many a ' job' is prevented by this relentless criticism. The government proposal, it would now seem, was on the whole in the country's interest, but it had weak points. In attacking these the Opposition was led on to take up a position of hostility to the whole project, while the government was equally indiscriminate in defending every jot and tittle of the bargain. In any event, with the bitter rivalry of the Grand Trunk and the Canadian Pacific looming up, it is doubtful if it could have been possible to prevent this antagonism being reflected in the politics of a country where the issues are so largely economic issues.

That the government was right in deciding for private construction and operation, there has since been little question. To build and operate a pioneer road, to make the inevitable United States connections or extensions, to undertake the subsidiary enterprises and to enter into the flexible, intimate relations with producers and shippers necessary for success, were tasks for which government departments were not well fitted. With the traditions which has unfortunately become established in Canadian politics, there would probably be campaign contributions in the one case and graft in the other, but in the one case, also, there would probably be efficiency, and in the other red tape and stagnation.

As to what private company should be given the contract, there seemed more room for discussion. The members of the Howland syndicate were successful and substantial business men, and their offer appeared to be much better than the offer accepted. It was, however, denounced as a sham by the government forces, on the ground that its signers knew that there was not the faintest likelihood of the ministry failing to carry through the contract it had signed. How successful the Howland group would have proved we can only conjecture ; it is certainly not likely that they would have developed more courage, persistence, or enterprise than the men who actually carried out the project ; nor could they have fulfilled their obligations more fully and more honourably.

The parties differed, again, on the question of the Lake Superior link. The government urged the necessity of building at once an all-Canadian route, regardless of the added expense. The Opposition favoured such a route eventually, but urged that it was better for the present to make use of a road running from the Sault through Northern Michigan and Minnesota. Such a road would bring to Montreal the traffic of the American as well as the Canadian West. Then, when our West had been settled and traffic warranted, the task of cutting a road through the wilderness north of the lake could be faced, and meantime it would not be necessary to offer any company the extravagant terms necessary to induce it to assume this burden from the start. There was much weight in this argument, which Sir Charles Tupper himself had strongly urged only a few months before, and in the light of the later Canadian Pacific extension through precisely this American territory as well as through Maine, there was much buncombe in the flag-waving answer made. Yet, on the whole, so necessary to national unity was an unbroken road, so hard a country was this to make into one, that it was best to err on the side of safety. The political interests at stake warranted some risk of money loss.

It was, however, on the question of the form and amount of the aid offered that most controversy arose. Sir John Macdonald had lightly prophesied that in the end the road would not cost Canada a single farthing. He

doubtless meant that land sales would repay
the expenditure ; even this did not prove true,
and the statement awoke unreasonable expectations as to the bargain to be made.   When
the contract was made public it was denounced
as meaning nothing more or less than that
the country was to build the road and present
it gratis to the company.   To anticipate a few
years, we may note the actual results at the
end of 1885, when the last rail had been laid.
The cost of the main line only, including the
government sections, and of equipment, to
that date, was approximately $150,000,000.
From private sources some $50,000,000 net
had been secured : the $65,000,000 stock had
been sold at varying prices, realizing slightly
over $30,000,000 for the treasury, and first
mortgage bonds, land-grant bonds less amount
redeemed, and outstanding accounts made
up the balance.   The government, on its
part, had given, by the final arrangements,
$35,000,000 cash, and completed road costing
another $35,000,000 ; three and a half million
acres of the land-grant had been sold for about
$11,000,000, and at only two dollars per acre
the fourteen odd million acres left were worth
over $29,000,000.

On the other hand, it was urged that the aid

given was not so great as it seemed. The value of the government sections was particularly questioned.[1] Whatever its value, it was not more than enough to induce capitalists to run the great risks involved. The road had to be operated as well as built, and few believed that for years to come there would be sufficient traffic to make ends meet. Its future depended on the future of the West, and it needed a robust optimism at times to believe that the West would overcome frost and drought and other plagues. The fact that in 1885 Canadian Pacific stock sold as low as 33¾ in London, and a shade lower on this side of the water, shows the estimate the world of finance put upon the bargain it had made. Nor was the road completed in 1886. It was then only begun. Grades had to be bettered, trestle-work filled up, extensions flung out, terminals secured, and a new road built every few years.

[1] Giving evidence before the Senate Committee on Interstate Commerce in New York in 1889, President Van Horne stated that the company was obliged to abandon part of the surveys on which the government had spent millions, and make new ones; that the government sections were unwisely located, especially in British Columbia ; that the cost of the remainder was increased by having to join it to the unwisely located sections, and that, allowing for the saving which could have been made in location, he could have duplicated the latter for twelve or fifteen millions.

SIR WILLIAM CORNELIUS VAN HORNE

From a photograph by Notman

Looking back now, after the lapse of thirty years, it would seem that the government would have done better if it had given less of the land which was to prove so valuable, and had, instead, guaranteed the dividend on the stock for a term of years. In the eighties, however, western acres were held in little esteem and money guarantees, with Grand Trunk memories fresh, looked dangerous—and it was in the eighties that the decision had to be made.

More valid was the criticism of the remaining terms. The exemption from duties was wise, if inconsistent in a protectionist government, and the exemption from regulation of rates until ten per cent was earned had a precedent in a clause in the General Railway Act, not repealed until 1888, exempting all roads from such regulation until fifteen per cent on the capital invested had been earned. The exemption from taxation, however, was an unwarranted privilege, throwing undue burdens on homesteading settlers ; and the interpretation afterwards given that the exemption on lands extended until twenty years after the patent had been issued still further increased the difficulty. Objectionable, also, was the monopoly clause, barring United States connections for ten years. It was claimed that this exemption was essential if traffic was to be secured for the Lake Superior link, and essential also if capital was to be secured from England. The Englishman, one of the heads of the road declared, hated a monopoly at home as he hated the devil, but he looked with favour on monopolies abroad. The monopoly clause, as will be seen later, for a time did more to split East and West than the Lake Superior link did to bind them together in spirit.

But enough of discussion. Action came quick. Not a day was lost in organizing and beginning work.

George Stephen was chosen president, and held the post until 1888. To him more than to any other man the ultimate success of the Canadian Pacific was due. Indomitable persistence, unquenchable faith, unyielding honour stamped his character. He was one of the greatest of Empire builders. He never despaired in the tightest corner, and never rested while a single expedient remained untried. Duncan M'Intyre became one of the two vice-presidents, and took an active part in the company's affairs until he dropped out

in 1884.   Richard B. Angus came back from
St Paul to become vice-president and a member
of the executive committee.   His long banking experience and his shrewd, straightforward
judgment proved a tower of strength in days
of trial.

Donald A. Smith, while after 1883 a director
and a member of the executive committee,
took little part in the railway's affairs, though
at Stephen's urging he more than once joined
in going security when help was most needed.
James J. Hill left the directorate and unloaded his stock at the close of 1882, because
the company refused to accept his advice to
omit the Lake Superior section, and because
of the growing divergence of interests between
the St Paul, Minneapolis and Manitoba and
the Canadian Pacific.   With him retired John
S. Kennedy.   The Baron de Reinach also
withdrew at an early stage.   The English
directors, representing Morton, Rose and Co.
of London, retired as soon as the road was
completed, being replaced by representatives
of Morton, Bliss and Co. of New York.   E. B.
Osler came in with the Ontario and Quebec in
1884.   The board became more and more distinctively Canadian.

One of the first steps taken by the directors

was to open offices in Winnipeg, and put two men with United States experience in charge —A. B. Stickney, later president of the Chicago Great Western, as general superintendent, and General Rosser as chief engineer. The rate of progress was not satisfactory, and early in 1882 a fortunate change was made. William C. Van Horne, at that time general superintendent of the Chicago, Milwaukee and St Paul, and still under forty, was appointed general manager with wide powers. Some years earlier, when he was president of the Southern Minnesota, the leading members of the St Paul syndicate had had an opportunity of learning his skill. He had been in railroading since fourteen, beginning as a telegraph operator on the Illinois Central, and had risen rapidly in the service of one Middle West road after another. His tireless driving force was precisely the asset the company now most needed.

The first task was to find the money necessary to build the nineteen hundred miles remaining of the main line, to build or acquire necessary branches and extensions, and to provide equipment.

The government subsidies were the first

resource. The $25,000,000 cash and the 25,000,000-acre land-grant were to be paid as construction advanced. If the land-grant were put on the market at once, for sale to settlers, it would bring relatively little, in face of the competition of the free homestead land in adjoining sections. Three expedients were devised to make it available as soon as possible. An extensive campaign was begun to advertise the government free land and thus exhaust the supply along the railway line, and at the same time provide producers of freight. Bonds based on the security of the land-grant were issued to the amount of $25,000,000 ; $10,000,000 of this issue was sold in 1881 at 92, and varying proportions of the remainder were used as pledge for the government loans or execution of the contract. These bonds were redeemed and cancelled as the lands on which they were based were sold. Further, the Canada North-West Land Company was organized to buy five million acres for a long hold. The company included several members of the syndicate as well as some English investors to whom land appealed more than railway stocks. It found itself unable to handle this amount and the purchase was reduced to 2,200,000 acres. Sales to other companies and to individuals brought the total amount received or due from land by the end of 1885 up to $11,000,000.

Next came the contributions of the members of the syndicate and other private investors. The capital stock authorized was $100,000,000. In 1881 the members of the syndicate sub-scribed $5,000,000 at par. In May 1882 they allotted themselves $10,000,000 at 25. In December of the same year $30,000,000 was issued at 52½ to a syndicate of New York bankers organized by W. L. Scott ; this stock was eventually sold largely in Holland and in England. A final ten millions were pledged in New York and Montreal for a loan of half that sum, and later sold for about the amount of the loan. All told, sixty-five millions of stock had been issued and some thirty-one million dollars had been brought into the treasury.

Then the flow ceased. The brief gleam of prosperity which had shone over North America after the gloom of the later seventies vanished. Never had railway building been carried on so vigorously in the United States as in the years 1881-83, and the reaction was correspondingly severe. The collapse of the boom which had accompanied the first

operations in Manitoba, the failure of harvest
after harvest, the fading away of settlers and
speculators alike, robbed all but a persistent
few of faith in the Canadian North-West and
in the railway whose fortunes rose or fell with
it. The way of the Canadian Pacific was
made particularly hard by the manœuvres of
rival companies. Some of the United States
Pacific roads, awake to the seriousness of the
competition threatened, attacked it in the
New York market. The Grand Trunk, natur-
ally alarmed by the incursion of the new road
into its best paying territory in the East, used
all the power of its influential directors and
its army of shareholders in England to bar the
London market.

The financial policy adopted by the Canadian
Pacific was unique in the records of great railway enterprises on this continent. It was
simply to rely entirely on stock issues, to endeavour to build the road without incurring
any bonded debt. Not until the last year of
construction, 1885, were bonds based upon
the security of the road itself issued for sale.
It was doubtless desirable, if possible, to avoid
the reckless methods by which so many American roads had been hopelessly waterlogged by
excessive bond issues. The memory of the

St Paul and Pacific's six-million share capital as against its twenty-eight-million bonded indebtedness was fresh in the minds of the members of the syndicate. By keeping fixed charges low, while earning power was still uncertain, they lessened the risk of having the road pass out of the stockholders' control into a receiver's hands. Yet as bonds could have been sold more easily than stock, it increased the difficulty of finding the necessary capital. Even so, it came within an ace of succeeding.

In pursuance of this policy the management, faced with a hesitating market, decided upon a bold step. Late in 1883, acting in accordance with the advice of New York and London financiers, they decided to endeavour to make a market for the unissued stock by giving assurance of a dividend for a term of years. They offered to deposit with the government as trustees a sum sufficient to provide for ten years a dividend of three per cent on the $65,000,000 stock already issued, to be supplemented, if possible, by a further dividend out of current revenues, and they arranged to make similar provision for the remaining $35,000,000 as it was sold. Over half the $16,000,000 necessary to purchase this annuity was deposited with the government at once and security given for the early payment of the balance. Only success could have justified such a locking up of the funds urgently needed for construction, and success did not come, though for a time it seemed probable. The sudden smash of the Northern Pacific, just completed by Villard, brought the stock down lower than before the fillip had been given. With sixteen millions locked up or pledged the company was in a worse state than before.[1]

In this emergency Stephen and Smith and M'Intyre pledged their St Paul or other stock for loans in New York and Montreal, but still the gap was unfilled. They turned to the

[1] 'The payment to the government of $8,710,240, in advance, of secured dividends, has deprived the company for the moment of the means for continuous, vigorous exertion in construction, without enabling it to recoup itself by the sale of its stock, as was confidently and reasonably expected' (Letter of George Stephen to the government, January 15, 1884).

Speaking in parliament in 1885, Edward Blake declared that, omitting the last ten millions issued, the company had raised on stock $24,500,000, and, counting the next two dividend payments, they would have paid or provided for dividends $24,875,000. Already $7,000,000 had been paid out in dividends, members of the syndicate receiving $3,610,000 on their $10,000,000 investment. In other words, before the road was opened for traffic, every cent paid in by the shareholders would have been paid back or set aside for dividends, leaving not a dollar for building the road.

government, requesting a loan of $22,500,000, to be secured by a first charge on the main line. In return, they agreed to complete the road by May 1886, five years earlier than the contract required. The request at first was scouted by Sir John Macdonald. Parliament would not consent, and if parliament consented the country would revolt. Bankruptcy stared the company in the face when John Henry Pope came to the rescue. He soon convinced Sir John that if the Canadian Pacific smashed, the Conservative party would smash the day after, and the aid was promised. The Cabinet was won over, and Sir Charles Tupper, hastily summoned by cable from London, stormed it through caucus, and the loan was made.

The funds thus secured were soon exhausted in rapid and costly construction in the mountain and Lake Superior sections. The government's blanket mortgage on the road made it impossible to borrow elsewhere. So, after the Riel episode, to be noted later, a new arrangement was made with the government by which the $35,000,000 stock unsold was cancelled and an equal amount of first mortgage bonds issued. Twenty millions of this issue and the unsold lands were substituted for the government's security, and the remainder of the bonds sold at 95. This put the company once more in funds. The relief came none too soon. In one fateful day in July, when the final passing of the bill was being tensely awaited, the Canadian Pacific, which now borrows fifty millions any day before breakfast, was within three hours of bankruptcy for lack of a few hundred thousand dollars. But by March 1886 every cent of the company's obligations to the government was paid off, twenty millions in cash and the remainder in land at $1.50 an acre.

The men behind the Canadian Pacific proved themselves possessed of courage and determination such as will always win them honour. At more than one critical stage they staked their all to keep the work going. But the fact remains that the bulk of the resources utilized in the original building of the road were provided or advanced by the people of Canada. The Canadian Pacific is as truly a monument of public as of private faith.

Meanwhile, the work of construction had been going ahead. Under William Van Horne's masterful methods the leisurely pace of government construction quickened into the most rapid achievement on record. A time-schedule, carefully made out in advance, was adhered to with remarkably little variation.

Work was begun at the east end of the line, from the point of junction with the Canada Central, but at first energy was devoted chiefly to the portion crossing the plains. Important changes in route were made. The main line had already been deflected to pass through Winnipeg. Now a much more southerly line across the plains was adopted, making for Calgary rather than Edmonton. The new route was shorter by a hundred miles, and more likely to prevent the construction of a rival road south of it later. For many years after the Palliser-Dawson-Hinds reports of the late fifties, it had been assumed that the tillable lands of the West lay in a ' Fertile Belt ' or rainbow, following roughly the Saskatchewan valley and curving round a big wedge of the American desert projecting north. Certainly the short, withered, russet-coloured grass lands of the border country looked forbidding beside the green herbage of the North Saskatchewan. But in 1879 Professor Macoun's investigations had shown that the southern lands had been belied by rumour, and that only a very small section was hopelessly arid. With this objection removed, the only drawback to the

southern route was the difficulty of finding as
good a route through the mountains as the
northerly Yellowhead Pass route afforded, but
on this the company decided to take its
chances.

Work on the plains was begun in May 1881,
and by the end of the year 161 miles had
been completed. This progress was counted
too slow, and under Van Horne's management a contract was made in 1882, with
Langdon and Shepard of St Paul, to complete
the line to Calgary. Later in the year a construction company was organized, the North
American Railway Contracting Company, to
build all the uncompleted sections of the main
line for $32,000,000 cash and $45,000,000
common stock. This was really a financing
rather than a construction expedient, and was
abandoned within a year.

In this section the engineering difficulties
were not serious, but the pace of construction
which was demanded, and the fact that every
stick of timber and every pound of food, as
well as every rail and spike, had to be brought
a great distance, required remarkable organization. Three hundred sub-contractors were
employed on the portion of the line crossing
the plains. Bridge-gangs and track-layers

followed close on the graders' heels. In 1882 over two and a half miles of track a day were laid. In the following year, for weeks in succession, the average ran three and a half miles a day, and in one record-smashing three days twenty miles were covered. By the end of this year the track was within four miles of the summit of the Rockies.

The change of route across the plains had made it essential to pierce the Rockies by a more southerly pass than the Yellowhead. The Kicking Horse or Hector Pass, short but steep, was finally chosen, but here, as at the Yellowhead, to cross the first range did not mean victory. The towering Selkirk range faced the pass, as the Cariboo Mountains flanked the Rockies farther north. Until the rails reached the hills the engineers had found no way through them, and had contemplated a long detour to the north, following the winding Columbia. Then Major Rogers, the engineer whom James J. Hill had suggested to take charge of the location of the mountain section, following up a hint of Moberly, an earlier explorer, found a route, steep but practicable, across the Selkirks, following the Beaver river valley and Bear Creek, and then through Rogers Pass into the valley of the Illecillewaet,

and so through Eagle Pass to the settled location at Kamloops. Both in the Kicking
Horse and in the Rogers Pass gradients of 116
feet to the mile were found necessary, but
these difficult stretches were concentrated
within one operating section of a hundred and
twenty miles, and could easily be overcome
by the use of additional engines. Unique
provision was made against the mountain
avalanches by erecting diverting timbers near
the summits and building mile upon mile of
snow-sheds, over which the avalanches passed
harmless. As a result of these expedients and
of raising the road-bed across the prairies un-
usually high, the Canadian Pacific lost less
time through snow blockades than the great
railways of the eastern United States.

It was not until 1884 that the wilderness
north of Lake Superior was attacked in strong
force. Nine thousand men were employed
here alone. Rock and muskeg, hill and hollow,
made this section more difficult to face than
even the Fraser Canyon. In one muskeg area
to-day seven layers of Canadian Pacific rails
are buried, one below the other. The stretch
along the shore of the lake was particularly
difficult. The Laurentian rocks were the
oldest known to geologists, and, what was

more to the purpose, the toughest known to engineers. A dynamite factory was built on the spot and a road blasted through. One mile cost $700,000 to build and several cost half a million. The time required and the total expenditure would have been prohibitive had not the management decided to make extensive use of trestle-work. It would have cost over two dollars a cubic yard to cut through the hills and fill up the hollows by team-haul; it cost only one-tenth of that to build timber trestles, carrying the line high, and to fill up later by train-haul.

An unexpected test of the need of this section came before it was completed. Early in 1885 the government realized too late that serious trouble was brewing among the half-breeds and Indians of the North-West. Unless troops could be sent in before the grass grew, Riel would have thousands of Indians on the war-path, and a long and bloody contest and a serious setback to the West would be inevitable. The railway was far from complete, with a hundred and twenty miles of gaps unfilled, and the government considered it impossible to get the troops in in time. But Van Horne, who had had much experience in handling troops in the Civil War, did not have that word in his vocabulary, and astonished the authorities by offering to take men from Kingston or Quebec to Qu'Appelle in ten days. Part of the gaps were bridged by temporary rails laid on ice and snow, only ninety miles being uncompleted by spring. In one stretch the men were marched across the ice to save a long detour. Through the rest they were carried, covered with furs and straw, in contractors' sleighs along the tote-roads from one camp to the next. In four days from leaving Kingston the first troops landed at Winnipeg; and though the revolt was not prevented, it was speedily crushed. There was no longer any question about the value of the north shore link, and the opposition to the Canadian Pacific fell from that hour. It was even suggested that the company should build a statue to Louis Riel. As for the government, it could well claim that its persistence in pushing through this part of the road nearly offset its red-tape carelessness in permitting the rebellion to come to a head.

Meanwhile, the government section between Port Arthur, or rather Fort William, and Winnipeg had been taken over by the company in 1883, though not entirely completed. Two years later the thousands of Chinese

navvies working on the difficult Kamloops-
Port Moody section finished their task, and
the government work was done. The only
gap remaining lay in the Gold Range, and
here in the Eagle Pass, at Craigellachie, on
November 7, 1885, the eastward and westward
track-layers met. It was only a year or so
before that the Northern Pacific had cele-
brated the driving of the last golden spike by
an excursion which cost the company a third
of a million, and heralded the bankruptcy of
the road. There was no banquet and no
golden spike for the last rail in the Canadian
Pacific. William Van Horne had announced
that ' the last spike would be just as good an
iron spike as any on the road,' and had it not
been that Donald A. Smith happened along
in time to drive the spike home, it would
have been hammered in by the navvy on
the job. Six months later the first passenger
train went through from Montreal to Vancouver. The longest railway in the world
was open from coast to coast, five years
before the end of the time required by the
original contract.

To realize how great a work had been accom-
plished requires to-day some effort of the
imagination. The Canada the present genera-

tion knows is a united Canada, an optimistic, self-confident Canada, with rapidly rounding-out industries and occupations which give scope for the most ambitious of her sons as well as for tens of thousands from overseas. It is a Canada whose nine provinces stretch almost unbroken from ocean to ocean. But the Canada of a generation earlier was far other. On the map it covered half a con-tinent, but in reality it stopped at the Great Lakes. There was little national spirit, little diversity of commercial enterprise. Hundreds of thousands of our best-born had been drawn by the greater attraction of United States cities and farms, until one-fourth of the whole Canadian people were living in the Republic.

It was the opening up of the West that changed the whole face of Canadian life, that gave a basis for industrial expansion, that quickened national sentiment and created business optimism. And it was the building of the Canadian Pacific that opened up the West and bound it fast to the distant East. Certainly not least among the makers of Canada were the men who undertook that doubtful enterprise and carried it through every obstacle to success; and not least among the generations whose toil and faith have made possible the nation of to-day were the four millions of the Canada of the eighties who flung a great railway across the vast unpeopled spaces of a continent to the far Pacific.

CHAPTER IX

THE ERA OF AMALGAMATION

WITH the building of the Intercolonial, the Grand Trunk, and the Canadian Pacific, the main lines of communication from ocean to ocean were completed. In the decade which followed, the marked features were: the adoption by the Dominion government of a policy of aid to purely local roads, and the expansion of the two great private companies, partly by new construction and partly by acquisition of the smaller lines.

It has been seen that the policy of Canada after 1851 and of the Dominion after Confederation was to give assistance only to lines of more than local and usually more than provincial importance. During the first ten or fifteen years after Confederation promoters looked to province and municipality for aid, and did not look in vain. Soon the provinces outran their resources, and began to clamour for increased federal subsidies to meet the pressing charges. But the Dominion government concluded that, if it had to provide the money needed, it might as well give it direct, and secure whatever political credit the grants would entail. In 1882 it decided to embark on a new subsidy policy.

In that year Sir Charles Tupper, minister of Railways, introduced a resolution to grant a subsidy of $3200 per mile—sufficient to provide the hundred tons of steel rails required for each mile at the existing price of $32 a ton—to each of four carefully selected roads, one in each of the four original provinces. During the next year eleven subsidies were voted, chiefly to Quebec and New Brunswick roads ; in 1885 twenty-five were voted, and fresh votes were made every year thereafter. Many of the subsidies lapsed through failure to begin construction, but usually they were revoted. The payments made averaged a million dollars a year. The practice did not make for pure politics, and it often led to the construction of lines for which there was no economic justification whatever. Trusting shareholders were induced to invest on the unfortunately wrong assumption that the government had assured itself of the need and the potential profit of the line before endorsing it by a subsidy.[1] In the western provinces a parallel policy of aiding local lines was adopted in 1884, except that land instead of cash was offered, a policy maintained until 1894.

He who paid the piper then stood on his rights to call the tune. Acting upon the wide power conferred by the British North America Act, the Dominion government in 1883 sweepingly designated as 'works for the general advantage of Canada,' and therefore subject to federal control, not only the main lines of railways, but the branch lines then or thereafter connecting with or crossing these lines or any of them. The power thus claimed was not effectively exercised for some time. D'Alton M'Carthy repeatedly urged in parliament from 1880 onward the creation of a Dominion Railway Commission, but the opposition of the railways proved too strong for him. When in 1886 the United States set up its Interstate Commerce Commission, the

---

[1] One such company, the Caraquet, which was given $400,000 in subsidies, declared, in floating $500,000 in bonds in England, that the capacity of the road was taxed to its utmost, and that an immense traffic was in sight. At that time its entire rolling-stock consisted of two locomotives, one passenger car, two box and fifteen flat cars, and a snow-plough.

government moved and appointed a royal commission, with Sir A. T. Galt as chairman, to consider the general question. Their report noted the existence of many grievances and suggested specific remedies, but considered that until further experience of the workings of the English and American commissions was available, Canada's needs could best be met by an extension of the powers of the Railway Committee of the Cabinet.

It may be noted that in 1882 the selling of railway tickets by private persons, a practice known as ' ticket scalping,' was prohibited in Canada, though the railways were forced to buy the exclusive privilege of selling their own tickets by agreeing to redeem unused portions.

The original contract with the Canadian Pacific had provided for an eastern terminus near Lake Nipissing, in order to show preference neither to Montreal nor Toronto, either of which could make connections by independent roads. Similarly, we shall see, thirty years later, Moncton was chosen as a terminus of the National Transcontinental, to hold the balance even between Halifax and St John. It was, however, impossible for the Canadian

Pacific to accept as permanent an arrangement which left it halting in the wilderness, and depending upon possibly rival railways for outlet to the great cities and ports of the east. It had, in fact, been empowered in its charter to acquire the Canada Central and ' to obtain, hold, and operate a line or lines of railway from Ottawa to any point at navigable water on the Atlantic seaboard, or to any intermediate point '—terms sufficiently sweeping. Few were surprised, therefore, when the directors began a policy of eastward expansion, though many were surprised at the boldness and extent of the plans and the speed and masterful strategy of the execution.

The first and most obvious move was to buy out the Canada Central, extending from Ottawa through Carleton Place to Pembroke, and under construction westward to Callender on Lake Nipissing. This was done in 1881, and the road was completed two years later. Again, in 1881, the parent line of the Canada Central, the Brockville and Ottawa, was acquired, and three years later a controlling interest was secured in the stock of the St Lawrence and Ottawa, thus giving connection with the St Lawrence both at Brockville and at Prescott. Still pressing eastward, the Canadian Pacific next sought entrance to Montreal and to Quebec. The North Shore road, built by the province of Quebec, would most easily give the connection sought. The province was induced, in 1882, to sell to the Canadian Pacific the western section, from Montreal to Ottawa. At the same time the eastern section, from St Martin to Montreal, was sold to the North Shore Syndicate. The Grand Trunk, alarmed at this advance, attempted to block further expansion by securing, jointly with the Central Vermont, control of the latter section. But the Canadian Pacific had the ear of both the Dominion and the provincial governments, and threats of aid in building a parallel line forced the Grand Trunk to relinquish control to its great rival. Not yet content, the Canadian Pacific sought winter ports at St John and Halifax. It secured control of the South-eastern Counties in Quebec, built a short line through Maine to Mattawamkeag with the aid of a large Dominion subsidy, acquired running rights or control by lease over part of the old European and North American, and thus entered St John. In 1890 its eastern development was completed for a time by the lease of the New Brunswick Railway, which had recently absorbed nearly all the small lines in western New Brunswick.[1]

Meanwhile the management had been equally aggressive in obtaining feeders in central and western Ontario, the very heart of the Grand Trunk's territory. In 1881 the Ontario and Quebec was chartered, by interests friendly to the Canadian Pacific, to build a line from Ottawa to Toronto, by way of Smith's Falls. Two years later this company acquired leases for 999 years of three important lines, and transferred them, along with its own road, to the Canadian Pacific. The first of these lines was the Toronto, Grey and Bruce, the narrow-gauge railway which ran north to Georgian Bay; the second was the Credit Valley, extending from Toronto to St Thomas; the third, the Atlantic and North-West, a road with little mileage but most useful charter powers, used for the seaward extension. Later, a railway was built from St Thomas to Windsor. Thus the Canadian Pacific secured access to

---

[1] The earliest intercolonial project, a railroad from St Andrews north, was brought to completion in 1889 when a short road, the Temiscouata, was built, linking the Intercolonial at Rivière du Loup with the New Brunswick Railway at Edmundston.

Lake Ontario, Georgian Bay, and the Detroit river. Not yet content, it built a branch to Sault Ste Marie. Here connection was made with the 'Soo' lines, giving outlet to St Paul and Minneapolis, and with the several roads later combined to form the Duluth, South Shore and Atlantic. Both of these lines shortly afterwards came definitely under its control.

In the prairie West the Canadian Pacific had been promised in 1880 a monopoly of through traffic for twenty years. The Dominion government, it will be remembered, had agreed not to charter, nor to permit the territories to charter, any lines between the Canadian Pacific and the United States border, running south or southeast. Going beyond these terms, the Dominion endeavoured also to prevent Manitoba from authorizing the construction of any such road, and disallowed one chartering act after another.

From the outset this provision proved a source of bitter and dangerous strife. On the one side it was contended that without this clause the necessary capital could not have been secured and that faith must be kept; that the traffic of the West should go to build up the eastern provinces, which had made a vast outlay on the road, rather than a foreign country; that the rates of the Canadian Pacific were as reasonable as those of American roads; and that other causes than railroad monopoly were responsible for the slow growth of the West. But the West protested that the rates were exorbitant—otherwise American competition would not have been feared—pointed to the exodus of settlers and the discontent of those who stayed, and refused to be sacrificed in the interests of foreign shareholders or even of sister provinces. Undoubtedly immigration was deterred, and relations between East and West were seriously strained. Finally, in 1888, the Dominion government was forced to yield. The company's consent was secured by a bond guarantee for some necessary extensions, and the provision was repealed. The Northern Pacific was brought in by the Manitoba government, and competitive local roads were chartered, but in this period the control of the Canadian Pacific over the western field was not seriously called in question.

The task before the management to secure traffic for the great system thus built up was a difficult one. It was a greater achievement to operate the Canadian Pacific successfully

R.B.   M

than to build it. When it is realized that when the company began operation the number of white settlers between Portage la Prairie and Kamloops, within twenty miles of the line, could be counted virtually on the fingers of one hand, the difficulty of finding traffic may be appreciated. Sandford Fleming had estimated that the road could not pay until there were two million people in the West. Yet pay it did from the start. The company capitalized its scenery, and built up a paying tourist trade. When wheat was lacking, ends were made to meet by carrying trainload upon trainload of buffalo bones to eastern factories. United States traffic was carefully cultivated at both ends of the line. An active immigration campaign was carried on. Various industries along the line, from coal companies to flour mills, were helped forward for years. A loyal staff was built up, and by grace of efficiency the company pulled through until the lean days of the early nineties were over.

During this decade of extraordinary activity the Grand Trunk had been neither content nor passive. Offended by the incursions into its best paying territory, it fought its younger rival in parliament and on the stock exchange, but with no lasting success in either quarter. It was more successful in its own constructive policy of expansion. In 1879 it had made a good bargain by selling to the Intercolonial the branch from Lévis to Rivière du Loup, which did not earn operating expenses, and by expending the proceeds in buying an extension to Chicago, which enabled it at last to secure the through traffic from the West for which it had been in large part originally designed. Its great coup came, however, in 1882, when the onward march of the Canadian Pacific and the bitter experience of fruitless rate wars led it to purchase its old rival, the Great Western, with its Michigan extensions. The construction of the St Clair tunnel between Port Huron and Sarnia, completed in 1890, marked another forward step in its western territory. Meanwhile it had acquired, in 1884, the Midland Railway, itself a recent amalgamation of the Midland, running from Port Hope to Midland, with the Toronto and Nipissing, the Grand Junction, from Belleville to Peterborough, and the Whitby and Port Perry, effected by two enterprising financiers, George A. Cox and Robert Jaffray. Four years later it absorbed the Northern and Northwestern roads, which had acquired jointly a branch from Gravenhurst to North Bay, so that here at least the older road check-mated its rival, securing the very paying link between Toronto and the western lines of the Canadian Pacific.

CHAPTER X

THE CANADIAN NORTHERN

THE first quarter-century of Confederation failed to redeem the glowing promises and high hopes of the founders of the new nation. Much had been done : the half-continent from ocean to ocean had been brought into the fold of one union ; national consciousness was slowly growing ; great efforts had been spent in linking the scattered parts by railways and waterways. But still political unity and economic prosperity both lagged. The country was torn by racial and religious bickerings. In the East, the exodus to the United States bled the country white ; in the West, drought, frost, and the low prices of grain kept settlers away. Canadian Pacific stock, selling in the middle nineties at 35, registered the market's estimate of the future of the Canadian West.

Then, slowly at first, and soon with cumulative momentum, came a transformation.

World-wide causes worked with local factors to change the whole face of affairs. New discoveries of gold and rising prices gave everywhere a fillip to trade. In the United States the disappearance of free land set its farmers looking elsewhere. In Canada change of methods, or the favourable turn of a climatic cycle, enabled the lands of the North-West to prove their abounding fertility. The discovery of gold in the Klondike afforded good advertising for Canada if little more of permanence. In the government and in the financial, the railway and the industrial worlds there were men who rose to the opportunity : no longer was Canada's light hid under a bushel. The most was made of the alluring gifts she had to offer to men the world over who strove to better themselves, and the flood of immigration began.

The first result of the swarming of thousands to the West was a demand for new railways, to open up plain and prairie and mineral range, and to make connection with East and West. The building of the railways in its turn gave a stimulus to every industry. As in the early fifties and early eighties, this period of rapid railway expansion—much longer, however, than previous periods—was an era of optimistic planning and feverish speculation.

First to seize the golden opportunities were the group of men who built the Canadian Northern. Railway history offers no more remarkable record than the achievement of these few men, who, beginning in 1895 with a charter for a railway one hundred miles long in Manitoba, leading nowhere in particular, succeeded in building in twenty years a road from ocean to ocean, and in keeping it in their own hands through all difficulties and vicissitudes.

Yet it is not exactly correct to say that they began in 1895. A long apprenticeship had been served before that time. William Mackenzie and Donald Mann, the leaders in this group, had both been trained in railway construction. Both were Canadian-born; and had fared forth as youths to make their way in the world. William Mackenzie, born at Kirkfield, Ontario, in 1849, had been in turn school-teacher, country-store keeper, and lumberman before a contract on the Victoria Railway—part of the Midland—revealed his destiny. Donald Mann, born four years later at Acton, Ontario, near James J. Hill's old home, had been brought up for the Christian ministry, but by twenty-one he was foreman in a lumber camp. At twenty-five he joined in the first rush to Winnipeg, and next year he undertook the first of many contracts on the Canadian Pacific. William Mackenzie had also carried through much work for this company. In 1886 the notable partnership of Mackenzie and Mann was formed. The firm built the Calgary and Edmonton, the Qu'Appelle, Long Lake and Saskatchewan, the Canadian Pacific short line through Maine, and many minor railways. They developed capacities which made each the complement of the other—Mackenzie a master of finance, and Mann as successful in extracting a subsidy from a politician as in driving ahead the work of construction. Later Z. A. Lash, a shrewd and experienced corporation lawyer, joined them, and the three, with able lieutenants, carried through their ambitious plans without more than momentary pause, until within sight of the goal.

It was in 1895 that William Mackenzie and Donald Mann, along with two fellow-contractors, James Ross and H. S. Holt—it is noteworthy how many Canadians eminent in finance and industry found their start in the building of the Canadian Pacific—decided to buy some of the charters of projected western

roads then going a-begging, and to build on
their own account.   They secured the charter
of the Lake Manitoba Railroad and Canal
Company, carrying a Dominion subsidy of
6000 acres a mile for a line from Portage la
Prairie to Lake Manitoba and Lake Winnipegosis, and induced the Manitoba government to add a valuable guarantee of bonds
and exemption from taxes.   In 1896 running
rights were secured over the track of the
Manitoba and Northwestern from Portage to
Gladstone, and construction was pushed a
hundred miles northwest from Gladstone to
Dauphin.   Next year Lake Winnipegosis was
reached.   Then the partners looked eastward.
The coming need of the West was an outlet
from Winnipeg to Lake Superior, to supplement the Canadian Pacific.   Accordingly in
1898, under powers given by Dominion,
Ontario, and Minnesota charters, construction was begun both at Winnipeg and near
Port Arthur.   Three years later the line was
completed.   Meantime the earlier road had
branched westerly at Sifton, and by 1900 had
crossed the border into Saskatchewan at
Erwood; while in 1899, in amalgamation with
the Winnipeg Great Northern, chartered and
subsidized to Hudson Bay, the name of the

combined roads was changed to the Canadian Northern.

Then came the coup which first made the public and rival railways realize the ambitious reach of the plans of the new railway. It will be recalled that when, in 1888, the ban upon competition southward with the Canadian Pacific had been lifted, the Northern Pacific had entered Manitoba. It had gradually built up a system of three hundred and twenty miles, but had not given the competition looked for, dividing traffic with the Canadian Pacific rather than cutting rates. Now the parent line was in the receiver's hands, and its straits gave the Manitoba government its opportunity. It leased for 999 years all the Manitoba lines of the Northern Pacific, but decided it could not profitably operate them itself without connection with the lakes. The only question was whether to re-lease them to the Canadian Pacific or to the Canadian Northern. After a lively contest the younger road secured the prize. At a stroke it thus obtained extensive terminals in Winnipeg, a line south to the American border, branches westward through fertile territory, and a link which practically closed the gap between its eastern and its western roads.

The Canadian Northern had now become the third largest system in the Dominion, stretching from Lake Superior to Saskatchewan, with nearly thirteen hundred miles in operation in 1902. The feeders were extending through the rich farming lands of the West; the line to Port Arthur supplemented the Canadian Pacific, providing a second spout to the funnel. But this merely local success did not long content its promoters. They announced their intention to build from sea to sea. Transcontinental railways were then much in the air : the Grand Trunk, the Trans-Canada, the Great Northern all planned extensive projects. Reviving prosperity and new-found confidence were making a dollar look as small to government and public alike as a dime had seemed some years before. Aid might confidently be looked for—but by which aspirant ?

In 1902 and 1903 a junction of forces between the Grand Trunk and the Canadian Northern was proposed, and would have had much in its favour. The negotiators could not come to terms, however, and each road continued on its independent plan. Nothing daunted by the Dominion government's decision to recognize and aid the Grand Trunk,

the Canadian Northern turned to a policy of
piecemeal construction, seeking aid from the
provinces as well as from the Dominion.

Making hay while the subsidy sun shone
and the prosperity of the Laurier régime was
at its height, the Canadian Northern pressed
forward extensions, flung out branches, filled
in gaps on every side. The main line was
pushed westward to Edmonton in 1905.
Branch lines were thrown out freely in all the
prairie provinces. In Ontario the gap north
of Lake Superior was bridged by a line from
Port Arthur to Sudbury, not completed until
1914. Toronto and Ottawa were linked with
the western lines, and several feeders were
acquired which gave connection with Kingston
and Brockville. In Quebec the Great Northern,
running from Hawkesbury on the Ottawa to
Quebec City, was absorbed in 1902, and the
Quebec and Lake St John five years later.
By building a tunnel three miles long under
Mount Royal, an entrance was secured into
the heart of Montreal. Nova Scotia did its
part by lending money to another Mackenzie
and Mann enterprise, the Halifax and South-
western. The Inverness Railway in Cape
Breton and the Nova Scotia Central with
minor lines were built or acquired, giving the

Canadian Northern first place in mileage in the province.

The most difficult task still remained—building a third railway through the mountains to the Pacific. Surveys for a road from Yellowhead Pass to Vancouver by Sandford Fleming's old route were begun in 1908. By the aid of lavish guarantees and subsidies this last link in the transcontinental system was pushed to completion in 1915.

The financial and political aspects of this great enterprise were as striking as was the construction. Governments have many a time given lavish aid, promoters have often built roads entirely out of the proceeds of bond issues, financiers have dominated great railway systems by a majority or controlling interest in the stock. But never before did a group of men plan to unite, on such a scale, all three arrangements—to build ten thousand miles of railway without themselves investing a dollar and still retain control. The men behind the Canadian Northern not only planned such a project, but carried it through, displaying in the process, and at every stage of the undertaking, a mastery of political diplomacy, an untiring persistence, and great financial resourcefulness. They are.

therefore, entitled to a special place among the world's railway builders.

Their plan was simple in principle, if wondrously complicated in working out. It was to build the road by government subsidies and the proceeds of the bonds guaranteed by government, and to control the road by issuing to themselves, for their services of promotion and management, practically all the common stock. To carry out this audacious plan, political influence, public enthusiasm, and the confidence of outside investors in Canada's future were all required and were all forthcoming.

Dominion and province vied in aid. This aid took many forms. The Dominion had abandoned in 1894 its policy of giving landgrants, but the original companies which combined to form the Canadian Northern had previously been promised and later received over four million acres: up to 1914 about eighteen million dollars had been realized from the sale of parts of this land, and the grants unsold were worth at least ten millions more. In addition, Ontario gave two million acres and Quebec one-third as much. Cash subsidies were not wanting. The Liberal government of Sir Wilfrid Laurier voted something less than two millions in cash to aid in building the link between Winnipeg and Lake Superior. It declined to recognize or aid the extension to the Pacific coast; but in 1912 the Conservative government of Sir Robert Borden gave over six millions for this work, and in the following year fifteen millions more for the Ontario and western Alberta sections of the main line. The provinces were less lavish, Quebec, Ontario, and Manitoba offering all told six millions.

But it was neither to land-grants nor to cash subsidies that the Canadian Northern looked for its chief aid, but to government guarantees. This device, the main form of state aid given in our first railway era, had long been discredited by the unlucky fate of the Grand Trunk and the Northern guarantees, and had been sparingly used since. To the Canadian Northern its revival was chiefly due. It was a seductive form of aid: provided that the railway thus helped had good traffic prospects, the government stood little chance of loss and the railway greatly gained by the certainty of the sale of its bonds and the higher price secured. But, like other forms of the extension of public credit, such as the issue of paper money, state guarantees are difficult to keep within bounds, and compel ever-fresh extensions to save the old liability. So Dominion and province alike found. From 1903 to 1911, under Sir Wilfrid Laurier, the Dominion guaranteed bonds of the Canadian Northern system to the extent of fifty-six millions; from 1912 to 1914, under Sir Robert Borden, it endorsed the Canadian Northern's notes for forty-nine millions more. Nor were the provinces behindhand. Mainly in the seven years from 1908, the five westernmost provinces pledged their credit on behalf of the same system to the astounding amount of over one hundred and thirty millions, British Columbia leading; Nova Scotia made a loan of another five millions. Thus endorsed, usually as to both principal and interest, the bonds of the Canadian Northern were floated with little difficulty, so long as money was to be had at all by any seeker.

In the meantime, while the road was being built by state gifts and bondholders' lendings, the great bulk of the stock of the parent road and of the chief subsidiaries was conveyed to Messrs Mackenzie and Mann for their services in promoting and managing the system. This method of financing had its dangers. It meant that there was no large commitment of shareholders' capital, to secure support in difficulty and compel responsibility in management. It meant that the control of the vast enterprise was in the hands of a few men, unchecked by public inquiry or the criticism of independent shareholders—whatever that might be worth. It meant that with all the cash capital taking the form of bonds, any failure to make ends meet, any lengthened depression, would bring risk of the mortgage-holders' foreclosure and receivership—not merely the shareholders' waiting for a turn of the tide—except in so far as the burden could be shifted to the governments that had endorsed the notes.

In the early years, thanks to general prosperity and to the strategic location and careful management of the system, ends always met, and a little over, and funds were always forthcoming for fresh expansion. But early in 1914 a crisis arrived in the company's affairs. The mountain section particularly, what with the higher cost of labour and the unexpected engineering difficulties, was calling for tens of millions more ; the stringency in the world's money markets, following the Balkan Wars, made investors chary of even gilt-edged offerings. There were many

millions of subsidies and guarantees still to
come from the state, but they would come
only as the road was completed, and meantime construction had to be financed. The
partner-owners could not provide the ready
cash needed for completing the gigantic task.
The bondholders had no inducement to do
so unless further guaranteed by the state.
The western provinces were at last becoming frightened of the load they had already
assumed. There was only one resource, the
Dominion government. True, it had only in
1913 made a gift of $15,000,000 on solemn
assurances that not a cent more would be
needed. But, it was urged, the emergency
was real. The road could not be left hanging half finished, after all the millions already
spent. Canada's credit must be protected, and
so the government, after a lively struggle, put
through a positively last guarantee of forty-
five millions. In return it was given forty out
of the hundred millions stock to which the
capital was reduced, and took the right to
appoint one government director. Whether
this step meant that the government was now
going to share the control and the profits
of the company, or whether it meant that
it was henceforth to be saddled with the

responsibility for any deficits, was a point much in dispute. Later, the outbreak of war in Europe delayed, but did not altogether halt, the floating of the loan and the completion of the remaining links.

Meanwhile, the many subsidiary enterprises, which the example of the Canadian Pacific has caused us to think appropriate to the transcontinental railway, had been undertaken by its youngest rival. Fast steamers between Montreal and Bristol, grain elevators, hotels, express and telegraph companies, all brought grist to the mill. Hardly to be distinguished were the allied interests of the partner-owners — iron-mines in the Lake Superior district, coal-mines in Alberta and Vancouver Island, whaling and halibut fisheries on the Pacific, and lumber-mills on the British Columbia coast—all bearing some relation to the development of the railway system.

In 1896, a railway a hundred miles long, beginning and ending nowhere, operated by thirteen men and a boy! In 1914, a great transcontinental system practically completed, over ten thousand miles in length, and covering seven of Canada's nine provinces! The impossible had been achieved.

CHAPTER XI

THE EXPANSION OF THE GRAND TRUNK

In the eighties, it will be recalled, the activity
of the Canadian Pacific in the eastern province had stirred the Grand Trunk to an
aggressive counter-campaign. Line after line
had been absorbed, extension after extension
had been built. New life seemed to have
been injected into the old system. Holders
of even ordinary shares began to dream of
dividends.

The activity was brief and prosperity
briefer. Only in the golden days from 1881
to 1883, when the West was enjoying its first
' boom ' and railway construction was at its
height, did the policy of expansion justify
itself from the shareholder's point of view.
The year 1883 saw the high-water mark of
prosperity for the Grand Trunk ; for in that
year dividends were paid not only on guaranteed but on first, second, and third preference
stock. Not again until 1902 was even a

partial payment made on the third preference ; not until 1900, save for a fraction in 1887, was anything paid on second preference ; first preference dividends were fractional and occasional, and even the guaranteed stock dividends were passed time and again. The financial position of this great system in the middle nineties may be briefly summed up in the statement that securities of the par value of £16,000,000, which in 1883 had a market value of £12,000,000, were worth in 1894 only £3,500,000. The junior securities had become only gambling counters on the stock exchange.

Where did the cause lie ? There was not one ; there were several. The first was in capitalization. The line had been hopelessly over-capitalized to begin with, and the new acquisitions doubled fixed charges, while net receipts increased only ten per cent ; feeders had proved suckers.[1] Secondly, in the general commercial situation. The whole continent was undergoing a trying test of panic and depression, of low prices and industrial stagnation. For a quarter of a century after

---

[1] One recent acquisition, the Toronto Belt Railway, to meet a rental of $19,000 and working expenses of $22,500, had gross receipts of less than $5000 a year.

1873 the gloom had been broken only at brief intervals—from 1880 to 1883, and from 1887 to 1889. In 1893 the price of wheat fell to the lowest point in a century. The great Mississippi valley had been flooded with settlers, railway and steamship threw their millions of bushels on the world's markets, while the gold basis of prices failed to expand in proportion. Western farms were, it was said, ' plastered with mortgages '; one-sixth of the railways in the United States went into receivers' hands in 1893 alone. Free-silver agitators denounced the ' gold bugs ' of the east; Coxey armies marched to Washington. Another cause was in excessive competition. The St Lawrence was more accessible to shippers than ever, while the Canadian Pacific had cut into the best paying territory in Ontario. In the Chicago traffic absolute demoralization ruled—reckless rate wars were waged, agreement after agreement was broken, line was played against line by grain-shipper or by dressed-beef magnate. A final cause was in management. The attempt was still being made to manage a great railway from London, three thousand miles away. The Canadian officials had little independent discretion; interminable delays, lack of initiative, red

tape, nepotism, followed inevitably. Here
and there officials strove strenuously to better
conditions, but the odds were against them.
Practically no Grand Trunk stock was held
in Canada; it was not even quoted on
Canadian exchanges; Canadians regarded the
road entirely from the user's point of view.

The traveller and shipper had less to com-
plain of than the shareholder. The service of
the road had been greatly increased. The
mileage was large in proportion to population.
Rates were low. True, it was a rare event
for a Grand Trunk train to arrive on time,
but it usually arrived.

For these various ills corresponding remedies
were sought in turn. Drastic capital reorganization was discussed, but nothing was
done. Commercial prosperity could not be
revived by the efforts of a single railway. Competition was met by agreement after agreement, ' gentleman's ' and otherwise, but in
vain. The most hopeful resource lay in the
only remaining direction, change of management.

In 1895 Sir Henry Tyler resigned from the
presidency after twenty-three years of faithful
service. His place was taken by Sir Charles
Rivers-Wilson, who had a record of efficient

service on the borders of politics and finance. The new president and a committee of directors made a thorough investigation of the Grand Trunk, and recommended some immediate improvements. Their chief contribution to its success, however, was the discovery of Charles M. Hays.

The great rival of the Grand Trunk had pressed forward to prosperity under the driving power of an American general manager. The new administration decided that it, too, would look to the United States for a chief executive of the ruthless efficiency and modern methods which the crisis demanded. They found him in the man who had pulled the Wabash out of a similar slough of despond. Mr Hays was not quite forty when, in 1895, he was appointed general manager of the Grand Trunk. He had risen rapidly since the days when, a boy of seventeen, he had entered the office of the Atlantic and Pacific. At twenty-nine he had been secretary to the general manager, and three years later manager himself, of the Wabash.

His presence was soon felt. The staff realized, some with relief, some with consternation, that the good old leisurely days, the days of vested interests, were gone.

CHARLES MELVILLE HAYS

From a photograph by Notman

Many were pensioned, some were dismissed. In some cases American officials were imported to fill the vacant posts, to the patriotic discontent of the old guard. Equipment was overhauled, larger freight cars were ordered, and new terminals acquired. The main bridges on the road—the Suspension at Niagara Falls, the International at Fort Erie, and the Victoria at Montreal—were all rebuilt on a larger scale between 1896 and 1901. The double tracking of the main line from Montreal westward was continued, and many of the sharp curves and heavy grades of the original construction were revised. Elevators at Portland, Montreal, Midland, Tiffin, Goderich, Point Edward, and Fort William were built or acquired. Trains came in on time. The whole system was ' speeded up.'

Later changes in the administration may be briefly summarized here. In 1900 Mr Hays's five-year contract as general manager expired. At the same juncture a vacancy occurred in the presidency of the Southern Pacific, which had fallen on evil days, and Hays was offered and accepted the post at four times his salary with the Grand Trunk of $25,000 a year. A year later he was back again in Canada. There was not room in the

Southern Pacific for both Hays and Harriman, then in financial control, and the Grand Trunk directors seized the opportunity which the breach afforded. In 1909 the wide recognition of Mr Hays's great services led to long overdue increase of the authority of the Canadian officials of the road by his appointment as president, on the retirement of Sir Charles Rivers-Wilson. Three years later, with his projects for expansion still incomplete, he met a tragic death in the sinking of the *Titanic*. Mr Edson J. Chamberlin, who had increased his reputation for efficiency by his management for four years of the Grand Trunk Pacific, was chosen as successor in the presidency.

Fortune favoured the new administration from the start. The tide in the continent's business affairs turned soon after the new men took the helm. The long depression ended, prices rose, farmers met mortgage payments, factory chimneys smoked once more, traffic multiplied.

The first result of the improved conditions was the easing of the tension in railway relations. There was no longer a life-and-death necessity for rate-cutting and traffic-stealing. Rate wars between the trunk lines in the United States came to an end. On the

Canadian side peace was longer in coming. The rush to the Klondike in 1897 started a rate war between the Canadian Pacific and the Grand Trunk, with its American connections, which lasted nearly a year. In its course rates were cut in the east as well as in the west, and the Canadian Pacific sent its west-bound freight from Toronto by Smith's Falls rather than use any longer the direct line of the Grand Trunk to North Bay. Peace was patched up, but the Canadian Pacific shortly afterwards set about building a road of its own from Toronto north to its main line, thus threatening the Grand Trunk with permanent loss of western business, and providing it with one incentive toward the great westward expansion it was soon to undertake.

Along with prudent retrenchments went increasingly aggressive expansion, both east and west. It was one of the main objects of Mr Hays's policy to secure a hold on the rich traffic possibilities of New York and the New England states. Portland, the original New England terminus of the Grand Trunk, had not become the great commercial centre it once expected to be. The first further step was taken in 1899, when the Grand Trunk secured control of the five hundred miles of the Central Vermont, with which relations had been close for some years past. With running rights over a gap controlled by the Boston and Maine, this gave a line from St Johns, Quebec, to the port of New London, Connecticut; from this point connection was made by boat to New York, where valuable terminal docks were owned.

New London was not the final goal, however—Providence and Boston offered greater possibilities. But to seize them it was first necessary to break through the monopoly of New England land and water transport, which the New York and New Haven line had acquired, or to come to terms with the interests in control. At first the word was to fight. The Grand Trunk was received with open arms by the business men of Massachusetts and Connecticut, eager for competition in railways, and in spite of all the political influence of the New Haven, Hays secured a charter for his Southern New England Railroad, to run from Palmer, on the Central Vermont system, to Providence; a branch from Bellows Falls to Boston was also planned. Construction was begun on the Providence line in May 1912, but suddenly halted. The Grand Trunk management declared the halt due to financial conditions, but New England suspected a compromise with the New Haven. Probably the change in policy was mainly due to the change in management, the new administration setting less store on the extension than the Hays-Fitzhugh executive had done.

All these eastern activities, however, were overshadowed by the Grand Trunk Pacific scheme. It was not the first plan the Grand Trunk had formed for westward expansion. In the embryo days of the Canadian Pacific, it may be recalled, the government had offered to the old line the opportunity of carrying through the new one. Later, a connection with the Northern Pacific through Sault Ste Marie had been discussed, but Van Horne had forestalled this move. Still later an extension of the Grand Trunk from Chicago northwesterly, possibly through control of the Wisconsin Central, had been under consideration. Nothing came of these plans until the proved fertility and rapid settlement of the Canadian North-West, the improved position of the Grand Trunk in the money markets, and the threatened loss of traffic between Toronto and North Bay, lured and urged the new administration forward.

In 1902 Mr Hays announced that the directors were considering building a line from North Bay, through New Ontario westward, to a terminus on the Pacific at Port Simpson or Bute Inlet. It would be a line of the highest standards. Government aid, the announcement continued, would certainly be sought and expected.

Once more railways became Canadian politics. There was little doubt that the government would aid either this or some rival transcontinental scheme. Opposition to the lavish subsidy policy of the past had developed, indeed, but it was overwhelmed by the demands from every quarter for a vigorous forward policy. It was Canada's growing time, and new-born confidence spurred country and government on. But if the line was to be not merely a private enterprise, but in part a policy of state, then considerations of high politics and low politics alike came in, and compelled material changes in the Grand Trunk's scheme before it could secure government acceptance.

A road from North Bay west would satisfy the local demands of the western provinces, but would not satisfy the local demands of the East, or meet certain common national aspirations. Eastern, and particularly Quebec, interests, demanded that any new transcontinental should be built far to the north, opening up the wilderness between Hudson Bay and the Laurentian highlands bordering the St Lawrence. A Quebec company, the Trans-Canada, was in fact urgently seeking support for such a line, endeavouring, since patriotism is in Canada the last refuge of the promoter, to stimulate investors by stressing the military advantages of the remote route. Again, the Maritime Provinces protested against aid to a company to carry the traffic of the West to Boston and Portland instead of to St John and Halifax.

Sir Wilfrid Laurier, the prime minister, endeavoured to combine all these ends. His plan provided for a road 3550 miles in length, beginning at Moncton—a neutral point between the politically inconvenient rivalries of St John and Halifax—crossing New Brunswick northwesterly, skirting the Maine border, and on to Quebec City, where the St Lawrence was to be crossed by a great bridge. Thence it would strike westerly far to the north of existing settlements. From Winnipeg the previously proposed route was followed. The West would have the development and competition demanded, the hinterland of Quebec and Ontario would be opened, and the ports of the Maritime Provinces put on an equality with their American rivals. And since this vast project was much beyond the power of the Grand Trunk to finance, it was arranged that the road should be divided into two sections. The eastern, from Moncton to Winnipeg, was to be built and owned by the government and leased to the Grand Trunk Pacific, free for seven years and at a rental of three per cent of the cost for forty-three years following. The western, from Winnipeg to the coast, was to be built and operated by the company, aided by a government guarantee of principal and interest on the greater part of the bond issue.

The announcement of this plan in July 1903 led to a storm of controversy as fierce as that which followed the launching of the Canadian Pacific. The Opposition brought forward various policies, looking to a greater measure of government ownership; the minister of Railways, Andrew G. Blair, resigned in protest; rival railways opposed openly and sometimes by secret plot; two general elections were fought on the issue. But rarely is a government in Canada defeated on a proposal, sound or unsound, to spend untold millions, if the money is to be had at all. The agreement went through, with modifications, in the following year, and the building of the great northern road began.

The railway policy of the past twenty years is still on its trial, but some tentative conclusions may be ventured.

In the first place, it seems clear that a new transcontinental was needed, not only to open the West, but to develop the hinterland of eastern Canada. The rediscovery of a vast clay belt north of the height-of-land between Hudson Bay and the Great Lakes, its known resources in timber and pulp and its probable mineral wealth, as well as the farming areas of the western plains, and the forest, mine, and fishery wealth of northern British Columbia, all gave some economic justification for the adventure. Perhaps even stronger were the political considerations. Here, again, if railways were Canada's politics, it was not only because Canadians were materialists, but because they were idealists. They were determined that, in spite of geography and diplomacy, in spite of Rocky Mountains and Lake Superior wildernesses, Laurentian plateaus and Maine intrusions,

Canada should be made one and independent. Often this national spirit has been manipulated to serve sordid ends in railway as in tariff matters ; the flag has covered a multitude of sinners. Yet whether it was the Grand Trunk or the Intercolonial, the Canadian Pacific or the Grand Trunk Pacific, the national purpose has been strong, and must fairly be set on the assets side of the sheet. Sir Wilfrid Laurier and Sir John Macdonald both worked with high courage and enduring faith for a greater and more united Canada. Any one who looked at a map of the Dominion and realized how incredibly narrow a fringe of population was strung out on the southern border, could not but feel that some attempt to add a second storey to the structure, to give breadth as well as length, was a national necessity. Perhaps least defensible was the Quebec-Moncton section ; true, it was essential, if freight was to reach the Maritime ports, that a shorter line with better grades than those of the Intercolonial should be secured if possible. Grades were bettered in the lines secured, but the saving in distance was not as great as old and incorrect surveys had led the government to anticipate.

How should the road be built, granted its

need ? Government ownership had its advocates, but experience of political ' machines ' and a recognition of the difficulties of a government line in carrying on steamship or irrigation or other subsidiary activities, or in making international extensions, told heavily against such a policy. The real choice lay between the two private companies, the Grand Trunk and the Canadian Northern, which were seeking to rival the Canadian Pacific. Undoubtedly the best solution would have been to amalgamate these companies, and thus to save the eventual outlay on a line north of Lake Superior, on closely parallel lines in the prairies, and on the enormously costly rival lines to be built through the Rockies. True, competition even in railway matters has still its merits, but one strong competitor of the Canadian Pacific would have better served the country than two in financial straits. This solution appeared for a time possible. As has been seen, negotiations were carried on in 1902 and 1903 looking to such a union, but unfortunately without result. Forced to choose, the government had no alternative but to give its aid to the older and better known system.

What standards were to be set for the

new road ?   The continent's pioneer traditions
were plain : build the road in the cheapest
way it could be made to hold together, with
sharp curves and steep grades if need be, with
scanty ballast, wooden bridges, and light
rails, since traffic would be light and capital
hard to get.   Then, if the country developed,
and perhaps after a reorganization or two,
rebuild the road on a permanent basis.   But
1903 was not 1873, and Mr Hays had learned
on the Wabash and on the Grand Trunk how
difficult it was for a second-class road to compete, and how costly was the process of re-
building with the line in operation.   He knew
that with high and rising wages for trainmen,
and with frequency of service a minor matter
on the long stretches, it was essential to concentrate loads in as few trains as possible, and
that a locomotive could haul almost twice
as great a load on a four-tenths grade as on a
one per cent grade.   So he determined to build
from the outset up to the highest standard,
securing a lower ruling grade than any other
transcontinental enjoyed.   The policy meant
high fixed charges and low operating costs.

What outlay would be involved and what
state aid was needed ?   Given the route and
the standard set, the outlay could not but be

vast. It proved, in fact, much greater than the estimates, as is the way with most big enterprises. The government section cost about a hundred and sixty instead of sixty millions, and the Grand Trunk Pacific section about a hundred and forty, or three hundred millions in all—twice the estimate for the Panama Canal and nearly its actual cost.[1] The standard set was high, and proved difficult to attain; labour was scarce and expensive, and prices of all materials were soaring constantly. The large expenditure lent colour to charges of corruption in the construction of the government section. Investigation after investigation was held, however, without revealing any gross betrayal of trust. One contractor had been handled too tenderly for repeated delays, possibly engineers sometimes stretched classification on a losing contract, and doubtless contractors were as usual given the privilege of contributing to party campaign funds. But, fortunately for the good name of Canada, the serious charges of corruption were not sustained.

[1] The Chicago, Milwaukee and Puget Sound, a high-grade road built to the Pacific coast at nearly the same time, was capitalized, it may be noted, at $157,000 a mile, or nearly $70,000 a mile more than the cost of the Grand Trunk Pacific and National Transcontinental.

Of this great outlay the country bore the lion's share. The Grand Trunk Pacific was organized as a subsidiary company of the old Grand Trunk, which secured control of ownership of all but a nominal share of the $25,000,000 common stock, given it in return for guaranteeing part of the Pacific bonds. Only $20,000,000 preference capital stock was provided for, and this was not issued. The interest of the independent shareholder was thus negligible. The money required was secured by the issue of bonds and debenture loans guaranteed by the government or the Grand Trunk. Up to 1914, in connection with the western section, the government had guaranteed the company's bonds to the amount of over eighty millions, had lent twenty-five millions for ten years at four per cent, and had made or promised a cash gift of twenty-three millions. On the eastern section, the company was subsidized by the use for seven years of the road, rent free, equivalent to thirty-four millions. It was a vast outlay, though not as difficult for the country to bear as one-third the amount would have been a generation earlier. The unique and consoling feature, so far as posterity was concerned, was that the bulk of the government expenditure was provided out of surplus current revenue, so that for the future the net income to be received from rental would much more than balance interest on borrowings.

Once the contract was ratified by parliament and by the Grand Trunk, and the new company had been formally organized with Mr Hays as president and Mr Frank Morse, and later Mr Chamberlin, formerly of the Canada Atlantic, as general manager, the work of surveying and determining the route began. On the government section political difficulties were met in New Brunswick, from the advocates of a route down the St John to the city at its mouth, and engineering difficulties of many forms in the long trail through the northern wilderness. The bridge which was being constructed by an independent company across the St Lawrence at Quebec collapsed in 1907, with great loss of life, and the delay in completing the second bridge made it necessary to depend upon car-ferries for some time. On the western section a good route through the prairies was decided upon, not without vigorous protest from the Canadian Pacific because of the close paralleling of its line. After repeated surveys of the

Peace, Pine, Wapiti, and Yellowhead Passes, the last was chosen, and a line was settled upon down the Fraser and Skeena valleys, passing through two million acres of fertile land. Remarkably low grades were secured; in fact, as favourable as on the prairie section. Kaien Island, 550 miles north of Vancouver, was chosen as the terminus, rather than Port Simpson as originally designed, and soon on its magnificent harbour and most unpromising site of rock and muskeg the new and scientifically planned city of Prince Rupert began to rise.

As the main line ran far to the north of the St Lawrence lake and river system, the original plan provided for the construction of branch lines to Fort William, to North Bay, and to Montreal. Of these only the first, aided by the Dominion and also by the Ontario government, was built. For the connection with North Bay running rights over the provincial road, the Timiskaming and Northern Ontario, sufficed. Later, in 1914, the Dominion government itself decided to build the Montreal branch. In Alberta and Saskatchewan over 1200 miles of branch lines were begun, under guarantees of bonds by the provincial governments. In British Columbia an independent road, projected by the contracting firm of Foley, Welch and Stewart—the Vancouver, Pacific and Great Eastern—promised when completed to give the Grand Trunk Pacific, by a traffic agreement, entrance into Vancouver.

The first contracts on the main line were let in 1905. For ten years construction went on, at the rate of a mile a day, with occasional slackening from scarcity of labour or financial stringency, but with no complete halt. Last to be completed were the section to be built by the company in the Central plateau of British Columbia and the section built by the government west of Cochrane. Meanwhile, the prairie lines had been in operation through to Edmonton since 1910, and grain reached Fort William over the Lake Superior branch in the same year.

From the beginning it had been questioned whether the Grand Trunk Pacific would carry out its bargain to operate the government section. The management professed its intention to perform every promise, but fulfilment was delayed. In 1915 the company demurred to assuming the lease, on the double ground that the road was not definitely completed, and that, since the change of government in 1911, the standard of construction agreed upon had not been maintained. Accordingly the government took power to operate the road from Winnipeg to Moncton, and to expropriate the company's branch from Superior to Fort William, pending further negotiations.

The great Canadian railway companies are much more than railways. The Grand Trunk system, in its new expansion, branched into every neighbouring field which could be made to increase the traffic. Fleets of steamers, on the Pacific coast, on the Great Lakes, and on the New England route, filled in gaps in its lines. Modern car-ferries crossed Lake Ontario and Lake Michigan, as well as the river Detroit. Elevators, it has been noted, were built at strategic points on the way from the wheat-field to the sea. Magnificent hotels were opened at Ottawa, Winnipeg, and Edmonton, with more rustic resorts in the parks along the route. Tourist traffic was stimulated by lowered fares and alluring advertising.

The Grand Trunk of 1914 was a much greater factor in the life of Canada than the Grand Trunk of 1894; it had become nation-wide in its interests, and had shaken off the unfortunate traditions of its earlier stagnant days. Difficult tasks still faced it : the building up of the traffic of the far north would demand ceaseless effort, and when the wheel of time should bring round slackened business once more, it would call for all its powers to make ends meet in face of rising wages, taxes, outlays of every kind. The record of the recent past gave assurance that the need would be met with courage and alert endeavour.

CHAPTER XII

SUNDRY DEVELOPMENTS

ALL the restless activity upon the part of its older and its younger rival did not rob the Canadian Pacific of the place it had held in the life and interest of the Canadian people. With a confident assurance based on the extent and the strategic location of its lines, the imperial richness of its endowment, and the proved efficiency of its management, it pressed steadily forward until it became the world's foremost transportation system.

The unbroken success and the magnitude of the operations of the Canadian Pacific in this period are almost without precedent in railway annals. By 1914 it had under its control more than eighteen thousand miles of railway, or more than six times the length of the original transcontinental line. It gave employment directly to ninety thousand men, whose monthly pay-roll reached five million dollars, and indirectly maintained many more, justifying the boast of its president in 1907 that directly or indirectly one-twelfth of the people of Canada received their income from the Canadian Pacific. In 1913 alone, the supreme year of Canadian railway expansion, the Canadian Pacific appropriated for new construction and betterments, equipment, terminal facilities, steamships and hotels, shops and elevators, nearly one hundred million dollars, or more than the original cost of the road. It touched the life of the nation at every conceivable point. From Atlantic to Pacific there was scarcely a town of any importance that was not reached by its lines. But its position was not merely national. It controlled over five thousand miles of railways in the United States, taking rank amongst the foremost systems of the Republic. Its steamship lines stretched more than half-way round the world, and in Liverpool and Trieste, Hong-Kong and Yokohama and Sydney, the red-and-white house flag of the Canadian Pacific made the company and the country known.

The management of the Canadian Pacific showed stability and continuity. It trained up in its own ranks the men for its highest posts. Sir George Stephen, later Lord Mount

Stephen, on resigning the presidency in 1888, had been succeeded by Mr, afterwards Sir, William C. Van Horne. As general manager, and then for eleven years as president, Van Horne carried the road through its most difficult period. In spite of failure of crops, low prices, and the slow trickling in of settlers, he kept aglow his own faith in the West and communicated it to others. Indomitable courage, tenacity of purpose, breadth of vision, mastery of organization and detail marked him as one of the great railroad builders of the century. Even when he retired from the presidency, becoming for another twelve years chairman of the board of directors, it was only to find new outlets for his energy in building pulp and paper mills in Quebec and railways in Cuba; for though, unlike many millionaires, he had not narrowed into his own business groove, and could paint a picture as well as buy one, the call to action never failed to stir him.

When Van Horne came to the Canadian Pacific in 1882, he brought with him the man destined to be his successor, Thomas G. Shaughnessy, a young Irish-American still under thirty, who had been engaged in railway work since he was sixteen. Appointed general purchasing agent, he rose rapidly, becoming president in 1899 and chairman of the board in 1911. Sir Thomas Shaughnessy maintained the progressive policy and the honourable record of straightforward management which has distinguished the Canadian Pacific—a railway singularly free from the questionable manipulations which have brought so many great American systems to bankruptcy. Other men left their impress on the road : men like Sir William Whyte, for over twenty years in charge of the western lines, David M'Nicoll, and George M. Bosworth and many others, gave most effective service.

After the first hurried staking out of the claim was over, by 1890, the Canadian Pacific refrained from further expansion until about 1898 : between these years only three hundred miles were added to the system. Then reviving prosperity and the activity of rival roads led to a new period of expansion. The additions made in this time can best be realized by a glance at the map (opposite next page). The most important may be noted briefly, beginning at the Pacific coast.

On Vancouver Island, the Esquimalt and Nanaimo Railway, which had been projected originally when it was hoped that Canada's first transcontinental would find its terminus at Victoria by crossing the straits from Bute Inlet, was acquired from the Dunsmuir interests. On the mainland of British Columbia activity was concentrated in the southern section. The rich mineral discoveries in the Boundary country led to the extension of the Canadian Pacific westward from Lethbridge, through the Crow's Nest Pass. The company was given a Dominion subsidy, and in return a general reduction of rates was secured. After years of contention with the Hill roads which were crowding into the same territory, and in face of immense engineering difficulties, a continuation of this line by way of Penticton gave promise of a second through route. Meanwhile, entrance was secured to Spokane and Portland in the United States. In the plains and prairie section a close network of lines developed. The narrow-gauge line of the Alberta Railway and Irrigation Company, which had done good pioneer service, under the guidance of Elliott Galt, in developing Alberta's possibilities in coal and irrigated land, was absorbed in 1911. The northern country was traversed by two new east and west lines. The Qu'Appelle, Long Lake and

Saskatchewan, extending from Regina to Prince Albert, lost to the Canadian Northern in 1906, was replaced by a new line and ' cutoffs ' and extensions built in every quarter. South of the border equal activity was displayed in throwing out feeders for the Soo and Duluth lines. The acquisition of the Wisconsin Central in 1909 gave the Canadian Pacific entrance into Chicago, while an agreement with the Wabash made it possible to link up its western United States lines with its southern Ontario road at Detroit. In Ontario, a branch from Toronto to Sudbury made the Canadian Pacific independent of the Grand Trunk's North Bay link, an extension from Guelph to Goderich tapped a fertile country, a line from Port M'Nicoll on Georgian Bay to Bethany near Peterborough gave a short through route for grain, a lake shore route eastward from Toronto provided access to the towns which the Grand Trunk, in its promoters' concern for through traffic or in its contractors' desire for low land charges, had side-tracked, while stock purchase and later a lease of the Kingston and Pembroke gave entrance into Kingston. In Quebec, short tentacles were pushed up into the Laurentian hills north of Ottawa ; south of the St Lawrence the chief step taken was the 999-year lease of the Quebec Central, sanctioned in 1912. In the Maritime Provinces the New Brunswick Southern or Shore line and the Dominion Atlantic, successor to the Windsor and Annapolis, were leased in 1911, and running rights secured over the Intercolonial into Halifax.

A marked feature of the Canadian Pacific policy from the beginning was the endeavour to control subsidiary or allied activities, and thus gain well-rounded independence. Its steamship lines came to girdle half the world. On the Pacific, service to Hong-Kong and Yokohama had begun in 1892 and to Australia in 1893, while a service on the coast from Seattle to the far north, and on the lakes of central British Columbia, followed. The Great Lakes fleet was still earlier in being. In 1903 the purchase of fourteen Elder-Dempster vessels ranging from five to eight thousand tons gave a whole North Atlantic fleet for seven millions, or the cost of a single *Lusitania*. It was soon increased by larger and faster boats. A line to Trieste, to secure a share of the immigration traffic from Eastern Europe, led to prolonged complications with the Austrian government early in 1914, on account of the hostility of German rivals.

Hotels followed steamships, some eight or ten being erected at strategic points from St Andrews to Victoria. Departing from the usual American practice, the company owned and operated its own sleeping-cars, and maintained its own express and telegraph companies. Its car-shops provided much of its rolling stock. Grain elevators were built at terminal points. In the later years a systematic policy of developing its western lands was adopted. A special department of Natural Resources was established, irrigation works were begun on a huge scale in the tract of three million acres between Calgary and Medicine Hat, and ready-made farms were provided or loans made to selected settlers.

The method of financing these countless enterprises was equally striking. Instead of increasing the proportion of bonded indebtedness, as was customary, the company sought additional capital chiefly by the sale of common stock. This procedure was possible because of the speculative value of the stock, based primarily on the growth of traffic, and of the value of the western lands still unsold : the dividend rose steadily to ten per cent in 1912, and the practice which prevailed until 1909 of issuing the stock at par gave holders valuable rights. In the latter year 125 was charged for the shares allotted, in 1912 150, and in 1913 175. As a result of the earlier policy an unnecessarily high price was paid for new capital, but fixed charges were kept low, and no great system was as safe from foreclosure. In 1914 the total assets of the company were valued at over $800,000,000.

Fifth in mileage among the railway systems of Canada is the group of fragments connected with the Great Northern Railway of the United States. James J. Hill had not been least among the members of the original Canadian Pacific Syndicate, but differences with his colleagues led to his retirement in 1883. Thenceforward he devoted himself entirely to the building up of the St Paul, Minneapolis and Manitoba, the railway acquired from the Dutch bondholders. Under the name of the Great Northern it had been extended by 1893 from Lake Superior to Puget Sound, and continued to grow steadily until, twenty years later, it controlled nearly eight thousand miles. The Great Northern was remarkable in at least three respects. Except for the original grants for the Minnesota lines, it was built through to the coast

without a dollar or an acre of subsidy from
the state.   Its capitalization was kept close to
the actual cost of the road and its fixed charges
were low.   It took the lead among American
roads in an aggressive and enlightened endeavour to build up the country through which
it ran, not only by flexible rate charges, but
by a direct campaign of education among the
farmers and other shippers on its route.

The mineral wealth of southern British
Columbia and the farming wealth of the
western plains turned Hill's attention toward
Canada once more about the beginning of the
twentieth century.   In British Columbia the
progress of the Great Northern invasion was
slow.   The character of the country made
construction difficult, and the Canadian Pacific,
appealing to national prejudices, fought every
inch of the way.   But Mr Hill pressed on.
The coal-fields of the Crow's Nest Pass, in
which he acquired a controlling interest, were
made accessible by a road from the south, and
a series of lines branching from Spokane
entered the Boundary mining region.   Winding in and out across the border the road continued westward to Vancouver.   Fortunately
duplication was in large part avoided; by
arrangements with the Canadian Pacific, the

Canadian Northern, and the Northern Pacific, the difficult country south of the Fraser was pierced by common lines, and common terminal facilities were secured. Meanwhile, in 1906 and 1907, more ambitious schemes were announced—the building of north and south lines through Brandon and Regina, and the construction of an east and west line from Winnipeg to the Pacific. In ten years, it was officially forecasted, the Great Northern would have as extensive a system in Canada as in the United States. What was more startling, Mr Hill denounced 'spoon-feeding,' and did not ask for a cent of subsidy. The building of the Grand Trunk Pacific and the Canadian Northern postponed indefinitely these larger plans. Actual operations were confined to the construction of branches running northward in Manitoba, to Brandon, Morden, and Portage la Prairie, and the acquisition, jointly with the Northern Pacific, of a lease of the Canadian Northern line from Pembina to Winnipeg, under the name of the Midland, and of terminals in Winnipeg. Meanwhile, as the map shows, branches from the main Great Northern line nosed up to the border at nearly a dozen other places.

The activities, real and projected, of the

Great Northern in Canada brought up acutely the question of the interrelations of Canadian and American roads. To some these activities appeared evidences of an infamous plot to drain Canadian traffic southward to United States ports and roads : to others they seemed to be philanthropic endeavours to rescue Western Canada from the clutches of monopoly. They were not, however, due to either political intrigue or knight-errantry, but to the same desire for profit which had led the Canadian Pacific to build up its great system in the western states. Other things being at all equal, it was of course desirable that Canadian traffic should follow Canadian territory to Canadian ports ; it was to this end that uncounted millions had been spent. Yet patriotism had a seamy reverse side of political buncombe. Every hint of outside competition in the preserves of railway or industrial corporations in Canada was denounced in interested quarters as dangerous and empire-smashing, while the counter-incursions into the territory of the United States were ignored or regarded as merely normal business enterprise.

As a matter of fact, in 1914 Canadian railways controlled four miles in the United

States for every mile in Canada controlled by railways of the United States. The Canadian Pacific alone owned or leased over five thousand miles in the United States, chiefly in the northwest, while it had close working agreements with the Wabash and the New York, New Haven and Hartford. The Grand Trunk controlled over seventeen hundred miles, two-thirds in the Michigan peninsula and the remainder in New England, while the Canadian Northern ran for some forty miles through the United States, south of the Lake of the Woods. The American interests in Canada were more scattered, but the Great Northern, the Michigan Central, the Père Marquette, and the New York Central all developed important Canadian extensions.

In short, the interrelations were certainly no more extensive than would have been expected in the case of two friendly nations lying side by side for three thousand miles, connected by ties of speech and by common commercial and social customs. The only difficulty which arose out of the situation was the division of jurisdiction between the Railway Commission of Canada and the Interstate Commerce Commission of the United States. The heads of the two commissions, Mr Justice

Mabee for Canada and Mr Knapp for the United States, endeavoured in 1910 to work out a plan for joint control, but without final success.

In the past half-century government ownership of railways has been much discussed in Canada, dividing attention with the allied question of railway ownership of the government. It cannot be said that any decisive public opinion or policy has resulted. Important steps toward government ownership have been taken in the last twenty years. The Intercolonial and Prince Edward Island Railways have been retained by the government and extended, a federal line has been built in Manitoba and a provincial one in Northern Ontario, and the National Transcontinental has been constructed by the government for lease to a private company. Yet, at the same time, the main railway projects continued to be entrusted to private companies, and the proportion of the whole mileage under private operation increased.

The most important incident in the Intercolonial's later history was its extension from Quebec to Montreal in 1898, by the purchase of the Drummond County Railway and the lease of a stretch of forty miles in length from

the Grand Trunk.   Six years later the Canada
Eastern, running from Gibson to Loggieville,
was purchased.   Many bankrupt lines in the
Maritime Provinces and Quebec were offered
to the Intercolonial as valuable feeders.   In
the later years of the government of Sir
Wilfrid Laurier and in the first years of Sir
Robert Borden's administration, authority was
sought to acquire such of these roads as might
be desired, but restrictions due to the action
of the Canadian Senate or the political diffi
culty of discriminating between the railways
prevented any rapid acquisition.   Changes in
administration were tried.   As a half - con-
cession to the demand that the Intercolonial
should be operated by an independent commission, a board of management was established in 1909, consisting of the chief officials
of the road.   In 1913 this board was dis-
solved and the management vested in a single
commissioner, F. P. Gutelius, formerly of the
Canadian Pacific.

Financial returns showed little improvement.   True, the record, unbroken since 1873,
of annual failure to meet even operating expenses, was varied after 1898 by small surpluses in two years out of three, but the net
deficits since Confederation rose to over eleven

millions by 1913; and while there was no question that the administration had been improved, there was room for belief that the surpluses had been in part book-keeping ones, obtained by including in the large capital expenditure items properly chargeable to revenue.

At first sight this failure to meet operating expenses, much less to pay interest on the investment, together with constantly increasing capital outlay, seemed to warrant strong condemnation of government methods. And, in truth, a serious indictment could be framed. Efficient government ownership is more difficult in a democratic country where shippers, employees, would-be employees, supply dealers, all have influence over the administration, than it is in a bureaucratic state. Intercolonial employees were given their posts and kept in them by political influence, and their numbers were often as excessive as energy was lacking. Supplies of coal and new land as required were usually purchased from political friends, with an additional margin for campaign contributions;[1] at election times the

---

[1] The deputy-minister, Mr Collingwood Schreiber, instanced in 1882 an attempt of a farmer, whose claim was nursed by influential politicians, to collect $70,000 for a gravel-pit liberally estimated to be worth $5.

road became a vast political machine. Under the administration of the governments of Laurier and Borden the grosser scandals ceased, but in one form or other political influence continued to be exerted.

Yet this was not the whole story. If the Intercolonial did not earn dividends, there were other reasons at work than government inefficiency. The road ran for long stretches through barren country where little local traffic originated. In competing for through traffic it was handicapped by the roundabout length of its route : it ran along two sides of a triangle, while the Canadian Pacific, subsidized by one political party, was built along the base, and the National Transcontinental, built by the other party, came in between ; in summer it had to face the competition of the St Lawrence route as well. Nor was dividend-earning the sole standard of success to be applied. The Intercolonial was built originally for political and military ends, not merely for commercial gain. It had given shippers the lowest rates in the world : ' the surplus is in the pockets of the people,' one of the political heads declared. If, it was often urged, the canals of Ontario and Quebec were operated by the government at a dead loss, without a cent of tolls, why grudge the Maritime Provinces, to whom Confederation had been less kind, the benefit of operating at bare cost the government railways! The Intercolonial had undoubtedly done much to weld the eastern and central provinces together, and this was worth more than a million dollars or two in interest charges.

The desire for rates at cost, or lower, which has made the people in Eastern Canada oppose all suggestions to turn over the Intercolonial to the Canadian Pacific or Canadian Northern, led those of Western Canada to urge government ownership of the other federal venture, the Hudson Bay Railway. Owing to its far northern position, Manitoba possesses ocean ports, Nelson and Churchill, which are nearer Liverpool than New York is. Why, then, carry the grain of the prairie fifteen hundred or two thousand miles to an Atlantic port before loading it on the ocean freighter? Proposals to build a railway to a Hudson Bay port and to establish a steamship line to carry the traffic at sea seemed plausible and won much western support. Investigation soon made the difficulties clear. Hudson Bay was fairly free from ice, but Hudson Straits were studded with icebergs far into the summer.

Ships of special construction would be needed for the dangerous passage, and, in any event, grain could not be shipped until the spring after it was harvested and would have to be stored in elevators during the winter. And in the meantime the three transcontinental railways were enlarging the eastern funnels, while the Panama Canal made an outlet by Vancouver feasible. Still, there was a gambling chance that something would come of a railway to Hudson Bay, and if the stroke succeeded, Canada would be given a new coast, and would front the sea at the north as well as at the east and the west. The territory between Le Pas, a terminus of the Canadian Northern, and Port Nelson, selected as the better port on Hudson Bay, had some mineral and agricultural promise. So, in the prosperous days of 1911, it was decided to attempt the work. As it was largely an experiment, the government's plan of state construction and possibly operation found wide support. The line was still under construction in 1914.

Another exploration road which amply justified the faith of its promoters was the Timiskaming and Northern Ontario. This railway, striking up from North Bay into the mineral region and clay belt beyond the height-

of-land, was begun by the Ontario government in 1902 as a colonization road. It was
fortunate enough to uncover the riches of
Cobalt's silver-camp in its construction; later,
mining development at Gowganda and Porcu-
pine brought it traffic; and the building of
the Grand Trunk Pacific made it an important
connecting link. It was able, then, from the
outset to show favourable results, direct as
well as indirect. It was built and controlled
by a government commission, efficient and
more or less free from politics.

CHAPTER XIII

SOME GENERAL QUESTIONS

WHEN the pace of construction slackened in 1914, Canada had achieved a remarkable position in the railway world. Only five other countries—the United States, Russia, Germany, India, and, by a small margin, France— possessed a greater mileage; and, relatively to population, none came anywhere near her. Three great systems stretched from coast to coast. Need still existed for local extensions, but by a great effort the main trunk lines had been built. Not only in mileage were the railways of Canada notable. In the degree to which the minor roads had been swallowed up by a few dominating systems, in the wide sweep of their outside operations, in their extension beyond the borders of Canada itself, and in the degree to which they had been built by public aid, they challenged attention.

While there were nearly ninety railway companies in Canada in 1914, the three transcontinental systems controlled more than eighty per cent of the total mileage. The variety of the subsidiary undertakings— steamships, hotels, express service, irrigation and land development, grain elevators—has already been indicated. The control by Canadian railways of seven or eight thousand miles of lines in the United States, with corresponding, if smaller, extensions into Canada by American lines, was an outcome of geographic conditions, intimate social and trade connections, and a civilized view of international relations which no other countries could match.

The aid given by the state had been remarkable in variety and in extent. In cash subsidies alone, up to 1913, municipalities, chiefly in Ontario, had given over $18,000,000 ; the provinces, in the order of Quebec, Ontario, Nova Scotia, New Brunswick, Manitoba, and British Columbia, double that sum; and the Dominion $163,000,000. Land - grants exceeded fifty million acres. Guarantees reached $275,000,000—the Dominion, British Columbia, Alberta, Saskatchewan, and Manitoba leading—with some sixty millions looming up in the year to follow. The privately owned railways of the Dominion were then capitalized

at a billion and a half; allowing for the
'water' in this capitalization on the one
hand, and for construction out of earnings
on the other, it may fairly be computed that,
omitting the guarantees, the state had contributed from one-third to one-half their cost.

The objections to this policy were manifold.
It had been one great source of rottenness in
politics. It had pauperized some sections of
the country, leading them to look to the
government to take the initiative in every
movement. The land subsidies had delayed
settlement, and the exemption of grants from
taxation had pressed heavily on the average
settler. The wealth of Canada tended to
concentrate in a few dominating groups.
Roads were built that were a sheer waste of
capital, useless for traffic or colonization, or
recklessly cutting into territory sufficient only
for existing lines. Yet the profits side of
the account was large. Settlement had been
hastened, transport facilities had been provided, values had increased, social intercourse
had been ameliorated, national unity had
been fostered, in ways impossible had private
enterprise been left to struggle on unaided.
In future, it might be hoped, private capital
could build unaided, or the state act directly.

In the allied field of government regulation progress had been made. Until very recent years, Canada had been more anxious to get new railways than to control old ones, and, besides, the worse forms of discrimination which stirred indignation in the United States had not been widely practised in Canada. But with the growing complexity of the industrial organization, and the recognition that competition could not solve the difficulties, a demand rose for more efficient regulation. The Dominion government, acting upon an able and thorough report by Dr S. J. M'Lean, established in 1904 a Railway Commission, permanent, non-political, and large enough to make it possible for its members, singly or jointly, to hear complaints in all sections of the Dominion. Later, telegraph, telephone, and express rates and services were added to its jurisdiction. Hampered by few of the constitutional limitations which have lessened the usefulness of the Interstate Commerce Commission, and guided by efficient businesslike heads—Blair, Killam, Mabee, Drayton—it soon established a unique reputation for fairness, promptness, and common sense.

But it is not merely in mileage or in relationship to the state that change has come in the three-quarters of a century since the first locomotive whistle was heard in Canada. Let us glance at some of the more striking changes in equipment and methods of operation. In the road bed, new standards of solidity have been set, grades cut down and curves straightened at a cost of uncounted millions, busy stretches double-tracked, steel bridges built in place of wooden trestles. The greatest single advance was the substitution, in the eighties chiefly, of steel for iron rails, making construction cheaper and repair easier, and permitting the running of heavier and faster trains. Heavier trains in turn brought heavier rails, eighty to one hundred pounds to the yard being the usual weight on main tracks, instead of forty or fifty in early days. Locomotives grew steadily in size from the *Kitten* of 1837 to the huge *Mallet* of to-day. Freight engines were differentiated from passenger engines. Coal was substituted for wood as fuel, and in some cases oil for coal. Electricity replaced steam in tunnels and other places where smoke was troublesome. The crude little freight cars, carrying four or five tons, gave way to cars carrying thirty tons or more, specialized for all conceivable purposes, from cattle and coal cars and oil tanks to refrigerator cars for fruit or meats or milk. Passenger coaches, following, as in other matters, American rather than English models, underwent a similar change, and improved steadily in size, strength, and convenience. The formal division into classes which marks European railway travel has not taken root in Canada; but between Pullman and parlour cars, first and second classes, the actual variety is great. Train dispatching, at first by telegraph, and latterly by telephone, has become a fine art; safety devices such as the air-brake, and more slowly block signals, have been adopted. The old confusing diversity of local time has been remedied by the adoption of a zone system, in consequence largely of the persistent advocacy of Sir Sandford Fleming. Thus the increase in mileage by no means represents the increase in service rendered: every year the engines grow more powerful, the cars larger and the trains longer, and the freight service more speedy and trustworthy. True, the service is still far from perfect, and when a heavy snowstorm paralyses traffic, or the diversion to new competitive building of money which should have gone into equipment brings about congestion, vigorous denunciation follows these brief reversions to the traffic conditions of the good old days.

There is no work that man has wrought that would give nobler and more enduring title to fame than the great cathedrals which mediæval Europe bequeathed to the world. Yet no man's name is linked with theirs. They were the work of generations, of an epoch, the expression of the genius and the labour and the worship of uncounted thousands. There is a whole world of difference between the mediæval cathedral and the modern railway, but this they have in common, that they are the work not of a few hands but of many, not a sudden creation, but the product of labours continued year after year. Leaders were indispensable ; we cannot forget the men who planned and the men who carried through and the men who organized the working of the great railway systems. Keefer and Fleming, Poor and Waddington, Galt and Hincks and Howe, Macdonald and Laurier, Mount Stephen and Strathcona, Van Horne and Hays, Shaughnessy and Mackenzie, these and many more, though often bearing feet of clay, we shall honour as builders of a mighty heritage.

But behind these loom up forgotten myriads who also were indispensable. The surveyor, often an explorer as well, striking out into the wilderness, braving sheer precipice and arctic blizzard in search of mountain pass or lower grade ; the man with the pick and shovel, a mighty and ever - shifting army— English navvy, Irish canaller, Chinese coolie, Swede or Italian or Ruthenian—housed in noisome bunkhouses, often fleeced by employment agent or plundering sub - contractor, facing sudden death by reckless familiarity with dynamite or slower death by typhoid and dysentery ; the men who carried on the humdrum work of every day, track-mending, ticket-punching, engine-stoking ; the patient, unmurmuring payer of taxes for endless bonuses—these, too, were perhaps not least among the Railway Builders of Canada.

BIBLIOGRAPHICAL NOTE

THERE are surprisingly few secondary books dealing with Canadian railway history available for the general reader. The admirable treatise by Dr S. J. M'Lean, 'National Highways Overland,' in vol. x of *Canada and its Provinces*, is much the best. Trout, *The Railways of Canada* (1871), and the article by T. C. Keefer in *Eighty Years' Progress of British North America* (1863), are useful for the early period, but are scarce. There is, however, a wealth of first-hand material —pamphlets, travellers' notes, company reports, Hansard debates, committee inquiries, and departmental returns. The largest collections of such material are to be found in the Parliamentary Library, Ottawa, the Library of the Department of Railways and Canals, the Toronto Public Library, and the Library of Queen's University, Kingston.

For progress from year to year since 1901, see Castell Hopkins, *The Canadian Annual Review*, vol. i *et seq*. See also, in this Series, *The Day of Sir John Macdonald* and *The Day of Sir Wilfrid Laurier*.

INDEX

Alberta, railways in, 184, 216, 224; grants in aid, 192, 241.

Allan, Sir Hugh, and the Pacific Scandal, 122-7.

America, North, ways of access into, 29-30; and transport development, 30-5.

Angus, R. B., and the Canadian Pacific Syndicate, 135, 136 n., 137, 151.

Ashburton Treaty, the, 57-8.

Blair, Andrew G., minister of Railways, 208.

Blake, Edward, his opposition to the C.P.R. contract, 143-5, 157 n.

Borden, Sir Robert, and the Canadian Northern, 191, 192.

Brassey, Betts, Peto and Jackson, railway contractors in the Maritime Provinces, 66-67, 69, 73, 75; in Canada, 70, 72-6, 79, 80, 81 and note, 83.

British Columbia, its terms of union with Canada, 115, 116, 128, 130; railway grants in aid, 192, 241.

Broun, Sir Richard, his railway, 58.

Buchanan, Isaac, promotes the Great Western, 47.

Canada, before the advent of the railway, 12-14, 19-26, 109-113; development of water transport, 14-16, 33-5; of land transport, 16-19; her railway policy, 27-30, 49-55, 64, 69-71, 169-72, 176, 190, 191, 209, 211, 233-9, 241-3; railway building, 36-49, 84-5, 93, 98, 182-3; the Grand Trunk, 71-74, 81-2, 83, 88-90, 94, 187; the Intercolonial, 106-8; the C.P.R., 116, 122-9, 139-50, 158-9, 164-5, 176-7, 224; a 'boom' period, 85, 181-2, 196; the Canadian Northern, 190-1, 192, 194; a period of depression, 197-8, 202; the Grand Trunk Pacific, 206-11, 213-15; railway interrelations with United States, 231, 232-3, 241; government roads, 108, 233-239; Canada's position in the railway world, 240-1. See Railways.

Canada Central Railway, 100, 128, 173.

Canada North-West Land Company, 153.

Canada Southern Railway, 40, 98-9, 104.

Canadian Northern Railway, 92; building of, 183, 185-9, 230, 232; financing of, 190-5; other enterprises, 195, 211.

Canadian Pacific Railway, the great demand for, 114-17; the

survey and route, 117-20, 129, 160-1, 162-3; the Pacific Scandal, 120-7; the syndicate, 130-42, 150-2; terms of building contract, 141-50, 172-173; financing of, 139-42, 147-150, 152-9, 181, 227-8, 236; its construction, 128, 159-68; development eastward, 173-175; further expansion, 175-178, 223-6, 232; and other railways, 139-40, 173-6, 186, 203, 215, 225; the world's foremost transportation system, 220-1, 226-7.

Canadian Pacific Syndicate, the, 130-42, 150-2.

Capreol, F. C., his ingenious financing scheme, 48.

Caraquet Railway Company, 171 n.

Cartier, Sir George, 107; and the C.P.R. contract, 123, 124, 125 n.

Central Vermont Railway, 101, 122 n., 174, 204.

Chamberlin, Edson J., president of the Grand Trunk, 202, 215.

Champlain and St Lawrence Railway, 36-8, 39, 40, 49-50.

Chandler, E. B., 53; his railway mission, 63, 65-6.

Cox, George A., 143, 179.

Elgin, Lord, governor-general of Canada, 72.

England, the locomotive contest in, 1-5; her lead in railway development, 7-10. See Great Britain.

European and North American Railway, 60-2, 64, 68-9, 102, 174.

Farley, Jesse P., and the Canadian Pacific Syndicate, 132, 137 n.

Fleming, Sir Sandford, 245, 246; and the Intercolonial, 56-7, 106-8, 117; and the C.P.R., 114, 117-20, 178.

Galt, Sir A. T., 172; his railway enterprises, 44, 45, 70, 71, 74-6, 77, 81 n., 84, 114, 246.

Gladstone, W. E., colonial secretary, 59.

Grand Trunk Railway, 38; building and financing of, 71-84, 87, 94, 95, 97, 99, 104-5, 122-3, 187, 232; and the C.P.R., 155, 174, 178-80; in low water, 196-9; changes of administration and material, 200-2, 218-19; eastern activities, 203-5; westward expansion, 205-6, 208, 211, 214. See Grand Trunk Pacific.

Grand Trunk Pacific, 205; the demand for, 209; question of the route, 207-8, 210, 215-18; building and financing of, 208-9, 211-15, 217.

Grant, Rev. George M., 117.

Great Britain, her railway mileage in 1846, 38; her railway policy in Canada, 54-5, 106; in the Maritime Provinces, 59, 60, 62-6, 73. See England.

Great Northern Railway, its development in Canada, 137-138, 187, 228-32.

Great Western Railway, building of, 40, 41, 46-7, 54, 55, 69, 70, 77, 84, 86-7, 91, 94, 95, 97, 99, 104-5; acquired by the Grand Trunk, 179.

Guarantee Acts, to aid railway building, 55, 69, 71, 84, 86.

Gutelius, F. P., manager of the Intercolonial, 234.

Gzowski and Co., railway contractors, 77, 81 n.

Hays, Charles M., 246; president of the Grand Trunk, 200-1, 203-4, 206, 212, 215; drowned in the 'Titanic' disaster, 202.

Hill, James J., and the C.P. Syndicate, 133, 134, 136 n., 137 and note, 141, 151, 162; and the Great Northern, 138 n., 228-30.

Hincks, Sir Francis, 52, 53, 246; his railway policy, 53-4, 56, 69, 70-1, 72-3, 88; and railway enterprises, 65-6, 73-6, 122.

Holt, H. S., and the Canadian Northern, 184.

Holton, Luther, his railway enterprises, 70, 71, 74-6, 81 n., 84.

Howe, Joseph, 52, 53, 246; his railway campaign in England, 62-4, 65-6, 69, 70; and state ownership, 66-7; his prophecy, 113.

Howland, Sir William, his railway syndicate, 143, 145.

Hudson, 'King,' railway promoter, 38, 47.

Hudson Bay Railway, 237-8.

Intercolonial Railway, 59-60, 98; building of, 105-8, 179; later development, 233-7.

Jackson, Henry, railway contractor, 73, 75, 76.

Jaffray, Robert, 179.

Keefer, Thomas C., a distinguished engineer, 36, 246.

Kennedy, John S., and the C.P. Syndicate, 132, 136 n., 137 n., 141, 151.

Kittson, Norman W., and the St Paul and Pacific, 133, 134, 136 n.

Lash, Z. A., and the Canadian Northern, 184.

Laurier, Sir Wilfrid, 246; his railway policy, 188, 190, 192, 207, 210.

Liverpool and Manchester Railway, 2-4, 36.

Mabee, Justice, chairman of Railway Commission, 232-3, 243.

M'Carthy, D'Alton, and a Railway Commission, 171.

Macdonald, Sir John, 246; and the C.P.R., 115, 116, 122, 124-6, 128-9, 130, 140, 141-2, 158, 210.

Macdonnell, Allan, railway promoter, 113-14.

M'Intyre, Duncan, and the C.P.R., 139-40, 141, 150, 157.

Mackenzie, Alexander, and the C.P.R., 127-8.

Mackenzie, William, 246; and the Canadian Northern, 183-5, 189-90, 192.

M'Lean, S. J., his report on railways, 243.

M'Mullen, G. W., and the Pacific Scandal, 121-2, 123, 124.

MacNab, Sir Allan, promotes the Great Western, 47, 53, 54, 55.

Macpherson, D. L., his railway

enterprises, 70, 71, 74-6, 81 n., 84, 123-4.

Manitoba, railways of, 176-7, 183, 185, 186, 233, 237 ; grants in aid, 191, 192, 241.

Mann, Donald, and the Canadian Northern, 183-5, 189-90, 192.

Maritime Provinces, their network of roads, 18 ; their railway projects and policy, 55-69, 93, 104 n. ; and the Intercolonial, 106-8, 237 ; and the Grand Trunk Pacific, 207-8.

Merritt, W. Hamilton, and the Welland Canal, 90-1.

Midland Railway, 100, 179, 183, 230.

Minnesota venture, the, 131-9.

Mississippi, transport development on the, 31-2.

Mitchell, Peter, and the Intercolonial, 107.

Montreal, and the St Lawrence and Atlantic Railway, 42-4, 60.

Morse, Frank, manager of the Grand Trunk Pacific, 215.

Mount Stephen, Lord, and the C.P. Syndicate, 134-7 ; and the C.P.R., 139, 140, 141, 150, 157 and note, 221-2, 246.

Municipal Loan Fund, the, 88-90.

National Transcontinental Railway, 172, 233, 236.

New Brunswick, railways in, 67-9, 102, 103 n., 175 ; grants in aid, 241. See Maritime Provinces.

Northern Railway, building of, 40, 41, 47-8, 55, 69, 84, 87-8, 94, 100, 104 n. ; acquired by the Grand Trunk, 179.

Northern Pacific Railway, 116, 121 n., 134, 157, 166, 177, 186, 230.

North-West Rebellion, the, and the C.P.R., 164-5.

Nova Scotia, railways in, 67, 102, 103 n., 188 ; grants in aid, 192, 241. See Maritime Provinces.

Ontario, railways in, 40, 41, 45-8, 49, 50-1, 80, 89-92, 98-101, 103 n., 175, 216, 233 ; and the C.P.R. contract, 123 ; grants in aid, 103 n., 190, 191, 192, 216, 241.

Osler, E. B., and the C.P.R., 151.

Pacific Scandal, the, 120-7.

Palliser, Captain, his mistaken view regarding a railway to the Pacific, 117.

Papineau, L. J., and state ownership of railways, 49.

Peto, Brassey, Betts and Jackson, 66. See Brassey.

Poor, John A., 246 ; his railway enterprises, 42-4, 60-1, 114.

Pope, John Henry, and the C.P.R., 139, 140, 158.

Prince Edward Island, its railway, 103, 233. See Maritime Provinces.

Quebec, railways in, 36-40, 41-5, 49, 92, 101-2, 103 n. ; grants in aid, 103 n., 190-1, 241.

Quebec and Richmond Railway, 75, 80, 81 n.

Railway Commission, the, 171-172, 243.

Railways, development of, 1, 4-

12, 244-6; the gauge question, 95-8; narrow-gauge lines, 98-100, 103, 224; wooden rails, 101-2; railway profits, 50, 79, 82, 86, 94, 95, 121; railway jobbery, 85-6, 170-1 and note, 213, 235 n., 236; grants in aid, 103 and note, 170-1, 241-2; 'ticket scalping,' 172. See under Canada.

Reciprocity Treaty, the, 80.

Richelieu, Cardinal, and the power of steam, 7.

Rivers-Wilson, Sir Charles, president of the Grand Trunk, 199-200, 202.

Robinson, Major, his railway survey, 59-60, 107.

Rogers, Major, his C.P.R. route through the Rockies, 162.

Ross, A. M., and the Grand Trunk, 77, 79.

Ross, James, and the Canadian Northern, 184.

Ross, John, first president of the Grand Trunk, 76.

Rosser, General, and the C.P.R., 152.

Ruskin, John, his opinion of the railway, 11.

Sage, Russell, and the St Paul and Pacific, 132.

St Lawrence, the canal system of the, 15-16, 34-5; river steamers of, 25.

St Lawrence and Atlantic Railway, 40, 41, 42-5, 54, 55, 69, 70, 75-6, 79.

St Paul, Minneapolis and Manitoba Railway, 128, 132, 134, 137, 151, 228. See Great Northern.

Saskatchewan, railways in, 184, 216, 224-5; grants in aid, 192, 241.

Scott, W. L., and the C.P.R., 154.

Shaughnessy, Sir Thomas, president of the C.P.R., 222-223, 246.

Simpson, Sir George, his record journey to the Pacific, 109-12.

Smith, Donald, 133. See Strathcona, Lord.

Stephen, George. See Mount Stephen, Lord.

Stephenson, George, his locomotive triumph, 2-5, 10.

Stickney, A. B., and the C.P.R., 152.

Stockton and Darlington Railway, 2-3, 6.

Strathcona, Lord, 112 n.; and the C.P. Syndicate, 133-4, 141-2, 151, 157, 166, 246.

Surrey Iron Railway, 6.

Taché, E. P., his railway advocacy, 65.

Timiskaming and Northern Ontario Railway, 216, 238-9.

Trans-Canada Railway, 187, 207.

Tupper, Sir Charles, minister of Railways, 139, 140, 141, 146, 158, 170.

Tyler, Sir Henry, president of the Grand Trunk, 140, 199.

United States, their transport development, 25, 32-3; competition with Canada for the western trade, 31-5, 39; railway development, 38, 52-3, 96, 115-16, 121; depression in,

198, 202; interrelations with Canada, 28, 50-1, 232-3.

Van Horne, Sir William, and the C.P.R., 148 n., 152, 159, 161, 164-5, 166, 205, 222, 246.

Waddington, Alfred, railway promoter, 115, 121, 122, 246.

Watkin, Edwin, his Pacific project, 114.
Watt, James, his reciprocating steam-engine, 9.

Young, John, his railway enterprises, 45, 65, 70, 114.

Zimmermann, Samuel, railway contractor, 47.

Printed by T. and A. Constable, Printers to His Majesty
at the Edinburgh University Press

THE CHRONICLES OF CANADA

Edited by George M. Wrong and H. H. Langton
of the University of Toronto

A series of thirty-two freshly-written narratives for popular reading, designed to set forth, in historic continuity, the principal events and movements in Canada, from the Norse Voyages to the Railway Builders.

PART I. THE FIRST EUROPEAN VISITORS

1. *The Dawn of Canadian History*
   A Chronicle of Aboriginal Canada
   BY STEPHEN LEACOCK

2. *The Mariner of St Malo*
   A Chronicle of the Voyages of Jacques Cartier
   BY STEPHEN LEACOCK

PART II. THE RISE OF NEW FRANCE

3. *The Founder of New France*
   A Chronicle of Champlain
   BY CHARLES W. COLBY

4. *The Jesuit Missions*
   A Chronicle of the Cross in the Wilderness
   BY THOMAS GUTHRIE MARQUIS

5. *The Seigneurs of Old Canada*
   A Chronicle of New-World Feudalism
   BY WILLIAM BENNETT MUNRO

6. *The Great Intendant*
   A Chronicle of Jean Talon
   BY THOMAS CHAPAIS

7. *The Fighting Governor*
   A Chronicle of Frontenac
   BY CHARLES W. COLEY

The Chronicles of Canada

PART III. THE ENGLISH INVASION

8. *The Great Fortress*
   A Chronicle of Louisbourg
   BY WILLIAM WOOD

9. *The Acadian Exiles*
   A Chronicle of the Land of Evangeline
   BY ARTHUR G. DOUGHTY

10. *The Passing of New France*
    A Chronicle of Montcalm
    BY WILLIAM WOOD

11. *The Winning of Canada*
    A Chronicle of Wolfe
    BY WILLIAM WOOD

PART IV. THE BEGINNINGS OF BRITISH CANADA

12. *The Father of British Canada*
    A Chronicle of Carleton
    BY WILLIAM WOOD

13. *The United Empire Loyalists*
    A Chronicle of the Great Migration
    BY W. STEWART WALLACE

14. *The War with the United States*
    A Chronicle of 1812
    BY WILLIAM WOOD

PART V. THE RED MAN IN CANADA

15. *The War Chief of the Ottawas*
    A Chronicle of the Pontiac War
    BY THOMAS GUTHRIE MARQUIS

16. *The War Chief of the Six Nations*
    A Chronicle of Joseph Brant
    BY LOUIS AUBREY WOOD

17. *Tecumseh*
    A Chronicle of the last Great Leader of his People
    BY ETHEL T. RAYMOND

PART VI. PIONEERS OF THE NORTH AND WEST

18. The 'Adventurers of England' on Hudson Bay
    A Chronicle of the Fur Trade in the North
    BY AGNES C. LAUT

19. Pathfinders of the Great Plains
    A Chronicle of La Vérendrye and his Sons
    BY LAWRENCE J. BURPEE

20. Adventurers of the Far North
    A Chronicle of the Arctic Seas
    BY STEPHEN LEACOCK

21. The Red River Colony
    A Chronicle of the Beginnings of Manitoba
    BY LOUIS AUBREY WOOD

22. Pioneers of the Pacific Coast
    A Chronicle of Sea Rovers and Fur Hunters
    BY AGNES C. LAUT

23. The Cariboo Trail
    A Chronicle of the Gold-fields of British Columbia
    BY AGNES C. LAUT

PART VII. THE STRUGGLE FOR POLITICAL FREEDOM

24. The Family Compact
    A Chronicle of the Rebellion in Upper Canada
    BY W. STEWART WALLACE

25. The Patriotes of '37
    A Chronicle of the Rebellion in Lower Canada
    BY ALFRED D. DECELLES

26. The Tribune of Nova Scotia
    A Chronicle of Joseph Howe
    BY WILLIAM LAWSON GRANT

27. The Winning of Popular Government
    A Chronicle of the Union of 1841
    BY ARCHIBALD MACMECHAN

PART VIII. THE GROWTH OF NATIONALITY

28. *The Fathers of Confederation*
A Chronicle of the Birth of the Dominion
BY A. H. U. COLQUHOUN

29. *The Day of Sir John Macdonald*
A Chronicle of the Early Years of the Dominion
BY SIR JOSEPH POPE

30. *The Day of Sir Wilfrid Laurier*
A Chronicle of Our Own Times
BY OSCAR D. SKELTON

PART IX. NATIONAL HIGHWAYS

31. *All Afloat*
A Chronicle of Craft and Waterways
BY WILLIAM WOOD

32. *The Railway Builders*
A Chronicle of Overland Highways
BY OSCAR D. SKELTON

Published by
Glasgow, Brook & Company
at 15 Wilton Avenue
TORONTO, CANADA

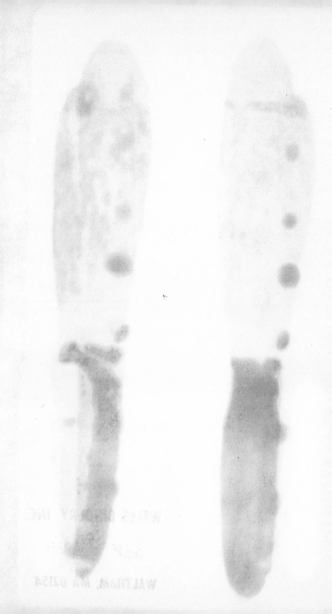

DATE DUE

GAYLORD	PRINTED IN U.S.A.